WAY OF

SO-BRR-470

ZING

A Guide to
Aligning Work & Life

Mark Gregory Nelson

Dr. William S. Silver

Way of *Zing*

Copyright © 2017 by Mark Gregory Nelson and Dr. William S. Silver

Editor, James Baldwin, WriteStuff Ink
Interior Design, Crissi Langwell, North Coast Stories
Book Cover and Brand Design, Kirk Gelardi, KDesigns

All rights reserved. No part of this book may be reproduced or transmitted in any form or by any means without written permission from the authors.

ISBN-10: 0-9992626-1-0
ISBN-13: 978-0-9992626-1-0

wayofzing.com

This book is dedicated to those
who have shown us what really matters.

Stacy, Aidan & Jack
Adrienne, Benji, Zach & Ari

Table of Contents

The Way Foreword

Surveying the landscape of your work and life, Zing Compass in hand, you stand confidently, staring at the Fourfold Path ahead of you.

As you gaze into lands of Prosperity, Discovery, Connection, and Meaning, you pause and reflect on all of the adventures that led you to where you stand today. You reflect on battles won and battles lost, relationships built and relationships soured, experiences embraced and experiences discarded, and wealth accumulated and wealth squandered.

Calmly gazing out into the distance, you take a deep breath, and a voice affectionately whispers. "It is all going to be okay. You know the Way."

You begin to walk forward. In some new and strange way, your life is beginning to make sense; you are beginning to understand. Through the deep reflection of your past, while awakened to the present, the path forward is becoming increasingly clear. Somehow, some way, all of the opportunities taken and missed, challenges faced and avoided, and choices made for better or worse, provide clarity. No longer a weight to be carried, these experiences serve as points of light on the path forward. They offer guidance, direction, support, and energy.

You realize that you are different than you were. Way different. The passionate energy inside is ignited; the energy of others is more evident. You see and hear things you never noticed, and begin to understand what really matters to you and others. And you know why.

You are traveling the Way of Zing.

Origins of *Zing* (About the Authors)

Way of Mark
By Dr. William S. Silver

The origins of *Zing* began formulating while Mark was serving as the President and Chief Operating Officer of the Nelson Family of Companies, one of the nation's top independently owned talent acquisition and workforce solution companies.

As an entrepreneurial leader of this hyper-growth company, Mark worked directly with some of the most distinguished clientele in the world. His energy focused in three key areas: identifying, attracting, hiring, and retaining top talent for the company and their clients, creating and leading innovative workforce management programs for those clients, and formulating first-in-class strategies to integrate the two. With this focus, he intimately understood, applied, and experienced the value of skilled, energized, and high-impact talent.

It was during this two-decade period at Nelson that the vision, ideas, and practices for Way of *Zing* originated. It was a time of massive structural change in the workforce, breakdowns of institutional career paths, proliferation of independent workers, and accelerated technological transformation and change. There were monumental shifts in how work got done, who got to do it, and the relationship between individual workers and their companies was being dramatically disrupted. These shifts were affecting the loyalty, commitment, and engagement between professionals and those they served, and affecting the way individuals viewed themselves, the work they performed, and the lives they wanted to lead. Mark took notice that significant amounts of human energy was being lost or destroyed along the way.

In this era of economic and social transformation, Mark became an alignment expert—an authority on the power of human energy. Through interviewing, counseling, coaching, and evaluating literally thousands of individuals, he developed a unique insight into how people worked and lived. These perspectives were further refined in subsequent roles as a strategy consultant, entrepreneur, and alternative asset investor. He was a "people person" in the "business of people," staring into the eyes of the masses, one person at a time. He had a firsthand lens into the soul of humanity, and the energy that drove it.

The Way of *Zing* is in part an observational derivative of Mark's intimate interaction with others, leading to many distinct discoveries—ones that are alarming, astonishing, and spark fear and wonder for the future soul, spirit, and sustainability of working professionals, and the very institutions they support.

What are these discoveries?

One, the number of people that are disengaged in their work and lives is startling. Too many people hate their jobs, hate their bosses, and feel little connection between their internal passions and their day-to-day work activities. Prosperous businesspeople are unhappy—living lives that are misaligned and out of sync with what really matters to them.

Two, accomplished professionals have become irrelevant—disconnected from what is going on and unable to offer real value to anyone. After storied careers, often in exemplary companies, they find themselves in situations of risk, and at times panic, finding that their careers are stagnant with little opportunity in front of them.

Three, recent college graduates and aspiring professionals are not ready for the challenges that work and life throws at them. Many lack passion, many lack purpose, and many lack the necessary universal skill sets and experiences to "get in the game." They have not received the appropriate guidance around exploring passion, skills, and ideals, and aligning purpose with economic reality.

Four, highly engaged workers feel that opportunity is slipping away from them, as they enjoy what they do but are unable to make ends meet. They are barely scraping by, piling up debt and obligations, and are not able to save for the future. They are not able to monetize their talents, and find peak career-earning time getting away.

Based on these discoveries, Mark surmised that for far too many professionals and aspiring professionals, finding work and a life that is in harmony with inner purpose and passion appears overwhelming, sometimes even hopeless. It can feel like an out-of-reach dream.

However, there is another group of people who are passionate, fulfilled, accomplished, and energetic—they have discovered a Way to align what really matters to them with the work they perform and the life they lead. They are in alignment, and have integrated their passion and purpose in all they pursue. They view their work/life as a platform for igniting and sharing passionate energy, and as an opportunity to share who they really are with what the world wants and needs. They are independent, confident, focused, and travel in many worlds, often simultaneously. They are life-long learners with an unquenchable thirst of curiosity, expanding their knowledge of themselves, their industries, and their market places. They are relentless connectors, continually identifying new and distinct ways to apply their value to the needs of others. And most importantly, they take responsibility for their work and their lives, proactively and incessantly driving towards all the things that matter to them.

It was this group of people that created hope, opportunity, excitement and energy around the future of work/life. It was these people from whom Mark drew to develop the Way:

"The Way of Zing has changed my life. I believe it can change yours.

Transforming how I view the world and my place in it, it directs and guides me in all I pursue. By assessing what really matters in my work and life, this work/life philosophy and process ensures the decisions I make and the moves I take, are meaningful to me, and those for whom I care.

The quest for alignment is deeply personal. At varying points in my life, I not only observed the struggles of others, I felt them. At times, I was them. These struggles ultimately led to a complete transformation of my life.

This personal transformation began one morning, ironically, in front of a mirror. I was reflecting on the countless people with whom I had engaged over the course of my career, assessing their trials and tribulations, successes and failures, and opportunities and threats. A momentary wave of panic struck me. Intently gazing at the half-shaven Mark Gregory Nelson, "successful businessman and entrepreneur," I stopped. I stared. I pondered.

Alarmed, in a flashing moment of despair, I thought to myself, "Am I one of them?"

That day, for the first time in my life, I clearly saw the real man in the mirror. Temporarily, I felt like I was a guest in my own body.

In truth, I was not one of them; I was all of them. While spending my life and career aligning the worlds of others, I let my work and my life go in and out of alignment. I realized that in my quest for professional progress and recognition, I had lost a part of myself. The decisions I had been making, and the actions I was taking, lacked focus on the things that really mattered. I had lost track of who I really was. My need to truly serve my family, my friends, and my biggest supporters subordinated to the calls of my professional life.

A week or so after this epiphany, I had another awakening. I noticed my life was, ever so slowly, beginning to change. My awareness was significantly more acute. I was beginning to observe and evaluate my feelings differently, as if they were separate from the deeper me. I was becoming more perceptive. I was beginning to ask myself questions that I now ask myself every single day.

Why am I engaging in this activity?

Why am I making this decision?

Why do I feel this way?

"Why?" had become my personal tunnel of introspection.

For years, these questions were subordinated as I pursued success, thinking that stability and security, and more wealth, respect and prestige, would somehow answer the questions. However, wealth, respect, and prestige alone did not. They certainly provided the liberation to freely explore myself and the world, but in and of themselves, they did not provide the answers I was seeking.

It was then when I stumbled upon the book, The Art of Happiness, *by the Dalai Lama, and my sense of real clarity began to emerge. The book was revealing and compelling; the origin of a personal journey which ultimately initiated these writings. That book sparked an energy inside of me, a quest for discovery and understanding, and a deeper truth—a truth that was bigger than the earthly treasures that the world had bestowed upon me. Discovery about the world and my unique place in it. Discovery about myself, and the ways I could better align my internal energies with what I needed from the world, and more importantly, what the world needed from me. Discovery about how I could better utilize my time, talent and efforts, for the benefit of others. Discovery about what really matters, by being the best father, husband, friend, colleague, mentor, and supporter that I can possibly be.*

The Art of Happiness *ignited a voracious appetite for books on philosophy, religion, and endless titles of self-discovery books. It also led me on a novel path, both literally and figuratively. John Steinbeck, F. Scott Fitzgerald, and Ernest Hemingway were staples. I was enjoying the fictional and non-fictional travels of others, a breeding ground for compassion and empathy.*

My quest, after all the years of aligning others, had become very personal and transformational. For the first time in my life, I was beginning to feel intimate with myself, and to understand the struggles of others more personally and deeply. Most importantly, I was beginning to be who I truly am."

Way of Bill

By Mark Gregory Nelson

Bill grew up in a family business. Silver's Drug Shop was a retail pharmacy located in the center of the small Southern Connecticut town of West Haven. Spending so much time engaged in one way or another with the family business, Bill found work and life inextricably intertwined. Conversation at the breakfast or dinner table inevitably turned to what was happening at the drug store. Activities, meals, and holidays—life—were scheduled around work hours and business cycles. Work was where he went to be with family and friends, where he went to learn, and where he went to help people.

This perspective of work being part of life, and life being part of work, was a foundation of the ideas that became the Way of *Zing*. For the next three decades, his academic and professional career would provide the training, research, and business experiences to articulate and develop this framework into a guide to help others live a life in alignment.

At his core, Bill is driven by the love of learning and by helping others learn. The excitement of discovery engages his mind. He is also an avid outdoor enthusiast. The mountains, forests, rivers, and trails replenish his soul.

As an honors student at the University of Michigan, and as a graduate business student at the University of Washington, he nourished his love for learning by immersing himself in classes, research studies, and consulting projects on leadership, organizational behavior, and business strategy. Simultaneously, he indulged his passion for the outdoors by spending time camping, hiking, biking, skiing, and backpacking. At twenty-five years of age, armed with a doctorate in business, the experience of working with companies across industry sectors, and the drive of a high need for achievement personality-type, he went in search of a place where he could satisfy both his work and life pursuits.

He landed at the University of Denver (DU) where they were redesigning business curricula so that students would not only learn technical business skills, but also graduate as better leaders and strategic thinkers. To give students the behavioral practice to grow their leadership talents, they pioneered the integration of outdoor experiential learning activities into the business program. Bill taught leadership in classrooms, and had students practice leadership by taking them rock climbing, rafting, orienteering, and sailing.

At DU, his career and life flourished as he discovered ways to integrate his life passions into work, and his work activities into life. His enthusiasm for skiing found an outlet in the University's Mountain MBA program, a customized hospitality business degree for the ski resort industry. His love of the environment led to advocacy for sustainable business practices, and he helped DU achieve top national rankings for incorporating environmental and social responsibility into their programs.

His curiosity for leadership effectiveness and organizational performance had him working directly with startup, mid-level, and global companies on executive and corporate education programs. His core value of "practicing what he teaches" motivated him to serve in a variety of leadership positions at the University, eventually becoming the Chief Operating Officer/Senior Associate Dean.

In 2008, he accepted a job as Dean of the College of Business and Economics at Sonoma State University (SSU). At Sonoma State, he found a place where he could integrate his entrepreneurial spirit and talents with an emerging interest in wine and wine business. He helped lead SSU's Wine Business Institute to a position of global leadership in wine business education and research.

Over the years, Bill has worked with dozens of companies, hundreds of executives, and thousands of students in the areas of leadership, strategy, performance, and personal effectiveness. A role model for the leadership and life practices he was teaching his students, the most important leadership lessons he taught did not come from his research, or from work with client organizations. They were the lessons of life taught to him by his son, Benji:

"There are moments in life that change everything—moments of pure insight, the moments that matter the most.

There is no going back in time from these moments, only the choice of where you go next.

I remember the moment when everything changed for me. It was three months and twenty-one days after my first son Benji was born. On that day, Benji was diagnosed with a rare form of Leukemia, a type of cancer that affects the blood and bone marrow, the spongy center of bones where our blood cells are formed. The disease develops when blood cells produced in the bone marrow grow out of control. Benji's leukemia had progressed quickly to a near fatal stage.

My wife Adrienne and I sat with the oncologist who told us, "We need to get your boy to surgery immediately." She handed us a sixty-page document listing in excruciating detail all the risks, complications, and probable adverse outcomes. She described a very complex course of treatment, and then went on to say that, even then, Benji had a small chance of survival.

No parent should ever have to hear the words "chance of survival" and his or her own child's name mentioned in the same sentence.

The next three years were extraordinarily difficult, and yet I have no right to complain. Benji did all the hard work. Chemotherapy. Total body irradiation. Experimental targeted drug therapy. Bone marrow transplant. As a parent, you watch your child go through these tribulations, wishing that you could trade places. Wishing that you could take the pain away. Wishing that you could make a difference.

What insight do you take away from watching your child almost die? What do you learn from watching him struggle to heal and recover?

I learned that every minute of life is precious—a gift to be cherished and celebrated. I learned that we should make every moment count.

Fast forward to the present. It is with a great amount of joy and relief that I can say my son Benji is an ordinary teenager who enjoys fencing, biking, hiking, playing video games, and disagreeing with his parents. However, he is also an extraordinary kid, because he is a cancer conqueror. Last year, Benji served as the Honored Hero for The **Leukemia & Lymphoma Society's Light the Night Walk,** *the organization's annual event to raise support and awareness for cancer treatment, research, and advocacy. I volunteered as the campaign's chair, and together we set out to give back to an organization that helped us in our time of crisis.*

It was an incredible experience for both of us, one with significant impact. We raised over a quarter of a million dollars, meeting together with businesses leaders, and speaking at schools, organizations, and conferences. We mobilized thousands of people to support the cause. We invested countless hours to make the walk a success. For each hour we gave, we received so much more in return.

For me, chairing the Light the Night Walk turned out to be a significant professional endeavor. As a business school dean leading a campaign to support the fight against cancer, I had the opportunity to connect with new networks of business leaders, casting the role of my business school as a supporter of community causes. I learned so much in the process, including the science of cancer research and treatment, running a grassroots fundraising effort, and staging a large-scale community event. Each discovery had relevance for my work as a dean. Learning things that I never would in the ordinary course of my job, I was making a difference and helping to save lives.

It was also an incredible, fulfilling venture. Working together with my son, I watched him mature before my eyes, from a boy into a young man. He was fearless as he got up in front of a room to speak, and relentless as he tirelessly worked for this cause. He took on the challenging disease of leukemia and transformed it into a positive experience, a badge of honor, and a source of strength.

One day, we were invited to be keynote speakers at the Sustainable Enterprises Conference, a large gathering of business and community leaders working for organizations focused on the triple bottom line of people, planet, and profits. I remember observing Benji with pride as he stepped up to the microphone, looked at the audience, and proclaimed, "My name is Benji Silver and I am a conqueror. I am a cancer conqueror, a survivor of a rare form of leukemia . . ."

As he shared his story and invited the audience to join him in walking to end cancer, a flash of inspiration hit me. Being there with Benji, participating in something that was important to my family and to many other families, I could no longer tell if I was working or living. I didn't know if I was there as Business School Dean, or Light the Night Campaign Chair, or Community Leader, or Proud Dad. I was just there, making the moment count, living a life in alignment. It was another moment of insight, one that I hope to share with you in the contents of this book.

I am inspired every day by my son Benji, and also by his brothers Zachary and Ari, and my wife Adrienne. No professional accomplishment can rival the fulfillment I experience spending time with my family. But I've learned that it doesn't have to. You can have both."

Interconnecting Ways – Our Story

Our lives collided many years ago at a business accelerator in Sonoma, California. We were both volunteering our time, and over a casual lunch conversation, we discovered that we held many common values, ideas, feelings, and beliefs. And, we had quite a few that were vastly different. We ignited and forged a deep connection over time. As fellow board members, business colleagues, team teachers, family friends, and now as the originators of the Way of *Zing*, we have invested thousands of hours working together on joined ventures. We have shared successes, failures, opportunities, threats, triumphs, and troubles.

Over time, as we explored the world of work and the workings of the world, we discovered a shared curiosity. We wondered why no one has created a practical work/life guide that combines external relevance and internal purpose. Why don't any of these great business doers and philosophical thinkers provide direction for creating an integrated work/life that aligns passion and purpose with the economic practicalities and realities of the world?

We learned that the answer to our question is rather straightforward—because it is difficult to do. It is difficult to talk about un-manifested energies, very personal inner passions and purpose, and give guidance on how to apply them. It is even more difficult to explain how to align those energies with practical steps in real life.

Our journey together to create such a guide became both the compilation of the *Way of Zing*, and an example of the results of the Way. As we worked together, developing and enhancing the philosophy and models set forth, our relationship deepened, and the awakenings we experienced together fueled our own *Zing* energy. Through a shared journey, with all its obstacles and challenges, we identified a road best traveled, together, a shared common purpose. That purpose was to be in service to you.

This book is a story written about you, for you. We have intentionally omitted examples and stories of others in our book so you can initiate an intimate dialogue with yourself, and ultimately, with those for whom you care.

The *Way of Zing* is a story about aligning your work and your life. It is a story about discovering what really matters to you, and the people you care about most. It is a story about living a life of purpose and relevance, where what the world needs from you is in congruence with who you are.

It is a mirror into the authentic you, a way to uncover, appreciate, and remind yourself who you are and what is important to you.

It is also a window into the world; a way to see the world with new perspectives, continuously refreshing, uncovering what really matters.

You may read the book straight through from front to back. You may read the book section by section or jump around. Put it down and pick it up. Set it on the table next to your bed and read a sentence or two each evening.

Ultimately, the *Way of Zing* is not merely a book to be read, it is a Way to live your life.

Introduction

Imagine waking up every day feeling inspired, passionate, and full of vitality, looking forward to the adventures the day will bring.

Imagine being truly valued by the world, making a difference to those for whom you care.

Imagine living a life where you are doing exactly what you are meant to do, pursuing all the things that truly matter in your work and in your life.

Are you living this life?

There is a Way . . .

We have all experienced times when the stars align, when everything springs to perfect order. These are days when we feel as if our lives are exactly as they are supposed to be—moments of real purpose, when what we are experiencing is the true manifestation of who we really are deep inside. Feeling highly valued, we are making a difference in the world, relevant to ourselves and to those with whom we share our lives.

For many of us, these experiences are all too fleeting— brief periods in time rather than enduring feelings. Often, working and living in harmony with our inner purposes and passions feels like a distant memory, an out of reach dream, or an unfulfilled wish.

Sometimes we are pulled in too many directions. There is too much to do, and never enough time to get it all done. What we do complete feels rushed, unfinished, and not our best effort. Our work commitments fracture our commitments to family and friends.

At other times, we have no direction at all. Overloaded and inundated with the noise of the world, we have little time to distill knowledge, know-how, and wisdom. Little time to assess what truly matters. There are too many decisions without clear and simple choices. We don't know what to do, how to do it, or why we are doing it at all.

We have competing priorities between passion and practicality, and we seek reconciliation between the two. We don't know whether to follow our hearts or to follow our heads. At the end of the day, we are left feeling completely drained—out of energy and running on empty.

There is a reason we are feeling this way. We are in the midst of a human energy crisis, a time when the forces of life are crashing together, testing us at every pass, and threatening to overwhelm us. Short on vitality and passion, we search for harmony and equilibrium between what we have to do to make ends meet, and how we really want to live our lives.

This is not the way life is meant to be.

There is a group of people who have found what we all are seeking. They love their work, are calling their own shots, and are having a lot of fun. Working for themselves while serving the world, they have discovered a Way to live their lives where work is not work. Work is simply part of who they are.

Always dynamic, their lives flow, repurposing, growing, transforming. Buoyed by unbounded curiosity, options are plentiful. Change is their opportunity. Vital, relevant, fulfilled, accomplished, and aligned—they love their lives. They are not making a living; living is making them.

They are work/life adventurers, traveling their unique paths of individual vitality, personal growth, shared intimacy, and world service. With warrior-like courage and Zen-like presence, they are living for today while building their tomorrow.

They are experiencing the Way of *Zing*.

Zing is the radiant energy of human vitality. It is the energy of stars aligning, when everything in your life feels in unquestionable congruence.

The Way of *Zing* inspires and empowers you to successfully navigate your work and life, pursuing your unique passions and purposes in ways that ignite work/life energy and vitality. Through the application of some simple yet profound practices, you can walk a Fourfold Path of awareness, alignment, action and actualization. An energy path leading you to a life of prosperity, discovery, connection, and meaning, the quadruple bottom line of human vitality.

You will matter, living a life of relevance and purpose, making a special contribution to the world.

At the end of the day, you will be energized, fulfilled, accomplished.

Traveling the Way of *Zing*.

Passage One

The *Zing* Truths

There is Zing –
The Energy of Human Vitality

There is a Cause of Zing –
Relevant Purpose

There is a Way to Zing –
Pursuing Prosperity, Discovery, Connection, and Meaning

Through the Fourfold Path of
Awareness, Alignment, Action, and Actualization

"Everything is energy and that's all there is.
Match the frequency of the reality you want
and you cannot help but get that reality.
It can be no other way."

Albert Einstein

1

Zing

Zing is the radiant energy of human vitality,
the energy of stars aligning,
when life feels in unquestionable congruence.

In our world, we encounter individuals who shimmer with radiant energy. They are full of vitality, achieving their most important dreams while making a difference in the world. They matter – to others and themselves. With warrior-like courage and Zen-like presence, they are living for today while building their tomorrow. They have discovered the Way of *Zing*.

Zing is the radiant energy of human vitality. It is the energy of stars aligning, of everything in your life feeling in unquestionable congruence. *Zing* manifests when your inner purpose and passions harmonize with external relevance and value, your inner life force uniting with the external world.

For many of us, the experience of *Zing* is fleeting, not an enduring state of being. For others, *Zing* is more than a passing sensation. It is the on-going conviction that you are doing exactly what you are meant to do, at a point in time, for a period of time, or over a lifetime.

Zing ignites when who you are deep inside aligns exactly with what the world needs from you, when the work you do and the life you lead are true manifestations of who you really are. Your inner purpose and passions are synthesized with external relevance and value. You are fulfilled, accomplished—you love your life.

When your *Zing* is unleashed, people will feel and experience your identifiable vital energy. You are highly valued and sought after, relevant to them, desired. People will want what you have. And they will want you.

Zing is the interconnectivity between our personal experience and collective consciousness. *Zing* can be joyously communal, reverberating through united relevance. It is the foundation of successful organizations, movements, and shared missions. More than ordinary passion for a cause or a goal, it is a powerful catalyst for collective purpose and competence.

Zing can be described with words, yet to truly understand *Zing*, you must experience it. Each descriptor or definition is just an echo of the true feeling. Reading a book about *Zing* helps point the Way, but to truly experience *Zing*, you must venture forth on new paths, seeking prosperity, discovery, connection, and meaning.

"Each of us must work for his own improvement
and, at the same time, share a general
responsibility for all humanity,
our particular duty being to aid those to whom
we think we can be most useful."

Marie Curie

2

Relevant Purpose

*All of our lives can and should have meaning to ourselves,
and be of value to others.*

*This is Relevant Purpose,
the foundation to living a life of Zing.*

The possibility of *Zing* resides within every single one of us. *Zing* ignites when your inner purpose and passions align with your external reality. Your life can and should have meaning to you, and be of value to others. This is Relevant Purpose, the synthesis of individual purpose and external relevance. It is the single causal factor for the creation of *Zing*.

Relevant Purpose manifests as your unique individual purpose provides benefit to others. When your true self—your deepest sense of who you are, who you want to be, and what you want to do and accomplish—is relevant to others, you are in alignment. *Zing* is unleashed in living a life of Relevant Purpose.

Purpose and passion are distinct, yet interrelated. Purpose is the core essence of who you are, directing you to destinations of intended design. Purpose provides you a reason and it anticipates a result. Passion creates powerful, compelling emotion and desire, an enthusiastic energy of expression and action, propelling purpose toward result. It is fuel for purpose. Purpose is a journey. Passion makes the journey all the worthwhile. It is the flame that powers fulfillment.

Purpose, which is wholly internally determined, is distinguished from Relevant Purpose when personal meaning is connected to external value. Purpose gives you the reason for living, and passion motivates you to execute it. Relevance connects your purpose and passions to the needs of others. These subtle but important distinctions are the key to keeping you relevant and making you valuable in today's fast-paced and ever-changing world.

You will know your purpose has value or relevance if people are willing to provide currency for that purpose. Currency may be financial, but other forms of exchange may have meaning to you, including emotional, social, physical, spiritual, and intellectual currencies.

Relevant Purpose unifies work and life, fueling your vitality. Work enriches life and life enriches work when they are joined together in harmony, not clashing in opposition. Your work/life becomes more fulfilling and more relevant, growing out of who you are, and who you need to be.

The beauty of Relevant Purpose is that it is never obsolete. It is a destination and a journey, evolutionary, always moving. All of life's outcomes can propel you down the path of your Relevant Purpose.

"Let us, then, be up and doing, with a heart for any fate; still achieving, still pursuing, learn to labor and to wait."

Henry Wadsworth Longfellow

3

The Four Pursuits

As we journey towards Relevant Purpose,
each step is important, offering an opportunity for
prosperity, discovery, connection, and meaning.

The Four Pursuits reveal paths where we invest our time,
and just as importantly,
reveal how we can live our lives.

The Way of *Zing* is a unique journey among and through the Four Pursuits of Prosperity, Discovery, Connection, and Meaning. Through these Four Pursuits, you will identify pathways to Relevant Purpose and ultimately to the unleashing of *Zing*.

The journey among the Four Pursuits is a work/life exploration of directed passion aligned with external opportunity. It is a distinctive, personal quest with many paths forward. The Four Pursuits help you determine where you are going. Any activity, work, project, pastime, adventure, or undertaking may be a path among the Pursuits.

Zing may ignite through an isolated Pursuit, but expands exponentially when the Pursuits are traveled simultaneously. One road can lead you to and through multiple Pursuits. Traveling in pursuit of prosperity, discovery, connection, and meaning, you ultimately realize multiple destinations, each unlocking a new adventure, creating more opportunities for you to explore Relevant Purpose.

Pursuits are not goals in and of themselves, but rather avenues to Relevant Purpose, the ultimate mission. If your journey is solely goal-oriented, you will be repeatedly chasing *Zing*, not fully experiencing it. You likely will find that there is always another goal to achieve, and then another, and soon you are chasing *Zing* instead of living it. As you journey towards Relevant Purpose, each step is important: an opportunity for prosperity, discovery, connection, and meaning. The Four Pursuits offer pathways where you invest your time, and reveal how you can live your life.

Your journey among the Four Pursuits is inherently an existential quest—a deep look inside yourself. You are a self-determining traveler, responsible for the authenticity of your choices. It is also an experiential quest. You are the explorer, the navigator, and the leader of your own expedition. As you encounter and engage, experience creates new insights, allowing you to grow, evolve, and step closer towards your Relevant Purpose.

You are the person in charge of your destiny—a destiny guided by the Four Pursuits of Prosperity, Discovery, Connection, and Meaning.

"Every effort therefore must be made to perpetuate prosperity."

Aristotle

The Pursuit of Prosperity

In Pursuit of Prosperity
we find our true selves
manifested in value to others.

Prosperity is the primary medium of exchange,
our unique relevance
shared generously with the world.

The Pursuit of Prosperity builds wealth to exchange with the world. It is a way to meet your basic needs while building and sustaining your relevance and purpose. In essence, you are taking care of yourself, developing the resources you need to journey through your life.

Prosperity is intrinsic and extrinsic wealth—the core of your personal asset and the principle value of exchange. It may encompass money, knowledge, love, skills, health, connections, experience, spirituality, meaning, or wisdom. Self-determined, only you can evaluate the amount and type of prosperity needed to support your Relevant Purpose.

What value do you have to offer the world?

The Pursuit of Prosperity generates the life-currencies necessary to discover, to connect, and to find meaning. It is difficult to navigate other paths successfully if you are not attending to your own needs and successfully guiding your own life. When you are both the cause and the effect of your own prosperity, you are independent, liberated, and free to travel each of the other Pursuits. Prosperity is the means for personal sustainability, allowing you to continue your work/life adventure indefinitely.

The Pursuit of Prosperity supports the sustainable, creative, and perpetually productive you, liberating you to align your changing purposes and passions with external opportunities. Prosperity enables the discovery of permanent relevance in an impermanent world, providing the means for the unconstrained repurposing of who you really are.

Do you tell yourself that you will be successful "when"—
when you are married,
    when you have children,
        when you make more money,
            when you get that promotion,
                when you are worth a million dollars?
The path to true prosperity is revealed when you stop journeying toward "when," and begin asking "why?"

Why do you want any of these things?

"Live as if you were to die tomorrow.
Learn as if you were to live forever."

Mahatma Gandhi

The Pursuit of Discovery

*The Pursuit of Discovery is infinite learning—
a commitment to experiencing new things
in new ways, in new worlds, always.*

*The world does not just offer us opportunity for discovery,
but demands it. We grow or we wither. We adapt or we
deteriorate. We travel or become sedentary.*

*As we discover,
we realize how much more there is to know,
summoning humility and awakening wisdom.*

Every minute of every day is an opportunity for discovery. Discovery is the pursuit of infinite learning and development, a commitment to actively seek out and experience new trails in new worlds. It is a Pursuit where you travel life's continuum, embracing impermanence, change, and the imperative of life-long transformation and growth.

Discovery is pursuit of the unexplored and uncharted, journeying to the unforeseen with comfort in all you do not know, coupled with confidence that someday you may. Searching for a deeper understanding, asking "why?" and then asking "why?" again, and then again. The best answers lead to new questions, the foundation of wisdom.

Discovery is a catalyst for life adventure, springing forth from awareness of your personal curiosity. Curiosity is inherently self-defining and insatiable.

What provokes your curiosity?

What knowledge makes you want to learn more?

What discoveries make you feel as if you know less than you did before, leading to new questions and motivating more curiosity and learning?

The Pursuit of Discovery is much more than the accumulation of new knowledge. It broadens awareness and insight, awakens purpose, deepens expertise, nurtures talents, and expands relevance. Discovery is self-knowledge as well as world knowledge. The Pursuit of Discovery is learning what you want to know, and what you need to know.

Each day presents opportunities to learn and grow. The Pursuit of Discovery is perpetual navigation into new realms. It requires you to engage, put yourself forward, and participate. It is freedom to join in, take risks, and evolve. A relevant and purposeful life is mostly an active life—a life of experiencing, expressing, and participating. To remain relevant, you must actively seek out these worlds, and journey to new places.

This does not mean you do not take time to catch your breath, or let your body, mind, and soul find refuge in quiet. To pursue discovery, there are times when you must pause, reflect, and be still to take the next step forward.

"We cannot live only for ourselves. A thousand fibers connect us with our fellow men; and among those fibers, as sympathetic threads, our actions run as causes, and they come back to us as effects."

Herman Melville

The Pursuit of Connection

In Pursuit of Connection,
we embrace and build a shared life,
blazing paths for others to pursue their relevant purpose
as we pursue ours.

Connection is more than helping people.
It is more than helping people help themselves.
Connection is helping people help others,
creating a virtuous cycle of endless possibilities.

The Pursuit of Connection is a journey of shared intimacy. In our interconnected world, Relevant Purpose requires more than simple self-sustainability. It requires others.

As you pursue connection, you embrace the vital thirst for human intimacy and shared experience. Selflessly giving and receiving, you travel with others, for others. You recognize people's accomplishments and offer celebration. You feel their suffering and offer compassion. With empathy and unconditional acceptance, you are here for others.

In a word, you care.

Because you care, you do not accumulate and hoard, but instead share and give, liberally and generously. Suddenly you discover a world that responds with the very gifts that you provide. Where you share knowledge, you garner more knowledge. Where you help others, they will help you. Where you trust, you will be trusted. Where you are a friend, you will find friends. Where you embrace love, love will envelop you.

Connection is a Pursuit of your Relevant Purpose integrated with the Relevant Purpose of others. *Zing*

expands through human interconnection, intensifying when relevance and purpose are pursued with others, awakening us to new and unforeseen opportunities for prosperity, discovery, connection, and meaning.

Prosperity seeks application. When you share your prosperity, you invest in the Relevant Purpose of others, and they in turn are investing in yours.

Discovery hunts for conveyance. As you share your discoveries, others learn from your experiences and surf your wake, traveling farther and deeper on their journeys.

Meaning thirsts for understanding. When you share meaning, you grow together, evolving ideas, beliefs, and values.

The Pursuit of Connection builds a community of shared experience and shared responsibilities, forging unique and special bonds that make life more meaningful. Connection ignites the synergistic power of creation.

Empathy creates understanding, strengthening bonds.

Dependability creates trust, building confidence.

Passion creates devotion, intensifying love.

Engagement creates contribution, fueling commitment.

Your journey towards Relevant Purpose is not only about where you are going. It is about those you travel with, and the people you meet along the Way.

At the center of your being, you have the answer;
you know who you are and you know what you want.

Lao Tzu

The Pursuit of Meaning

The Pursuit of Meaning is the guiding light
of Relevant Purpose,
helping us recognize and realize which paths of prosperity,
discovery, and connection we must travel.

Meaning is our personal North Star.

The Pursuit of Meaning guides you to actions that make you prosperous and motivates you to learn and discover, leading you to the connections you need and to those that need you. Meaning inspires you to act, transforming potential energy into kinetic energy and possibility into actuality. The Pursuit of Meaning is a path you travel simultaneously with each of the other Pursuits, adding clarity and significance to your prosperity, your discoveries, and your connections.

Meaning is more than how much you prosper. It is why you prosper. The prosperity you accumulate has the highest value when it is put to work.

Meaning is more than what you discover. It is why you discover. The discoveries you uncover seek application in real opportunities and challenges.

Meaning is more than the connections you make. It is why you connect with others. The connections you forge become meaningful when they are actualized, when "knowing someone" gives way to "doing with someone."

In pursuit of meaning, you are bound to ask "Why?" seeking not only answers, but also paths to new questions.

To pursue meaning is to see both inside and out, recognizing and realizing paths toward your Relevant Purpose.

Meaning is a mirror. It reflects your prosperity, discoveries, and connections, establishing what is really important to you—your purpose. It moves you from poor to prosperous, from curious to knowledgeable, and from isolated to connected.

Meaning is also a window, revealing where you are supposed to go and what you are supposed to do, thus catalyzing relevance. Meaning lights up your soul, making life brighter and better because you are making a difference and taking action in congruence with your Relevant Purpose.

In a word, you matter.

Meaning is found at the intersection of individual passion and collective need, where "I" becomes "we."

Individual accumulation gives way to collective advancement.

Personal knowledge becomes shared experience.

Intimate connections form a powerful community.

The Pursuit of Meaning unites us with everything that is bigger than ourselves, illuminating the Way to *Zing*.

*"If one advances confidently in the direction of his dreams,
and endeavors to live the life which he has imagined,
he will meet with a success unexpected in common hours."*

Henry David Thoreau

4

The *Zing* Compass

The *Zing* Compass is a reflection and direction tool to guide you on your work/life journey. The Pursuits are quadrants on the *Zing* Compass, helping you understand where you are, and where you need to go. They tell you where to focus your time and energy given your inner passions and external circumstances.

The *Zing* Compass can provide the answers for why you are taking a certain path, and which other paths you should consider. Why should you choose a particular course of action? Will you be doing this to prosper, to discover, to connect, and/or to create meaning? If the answer to "Why?" does not fall into one (or more) of the four quadrants, you should ask "Why?" again. And again. And if you do not know why and decide to do it anyway, you are certain to discover.

Zing multiplies on those paths that take you simultaneously toward all Four Pursuits.

How do you align your inner world with external reality and practicality, leading to a manifested life of Relevant Purpose?

Begin by calibrating your *Zing* Compass with the answers to three foundational questions:

Who are you?

Where are you?

Where should you go next?

74

These are questions of place and focus, the answers forming the basis for life's quests and adventures.

Who are You?

This is an exploration about your fundamental values, ideas, feelings, and beliefs.

Who is the essential you?

At this point in your life, how passionate are you about each of the Pursuits?

What is meaningful to you?

Only when you understand yourself at your personal core being is it possible to follow a work/life path that fulfills and matters.

Where are You?

This is an assessment of your current location and level of alignment.

How congruent are your present circumstances with your internal purposes and passions?

How aligned are your existing skill sets and recent experiences with the external world and associated demands for talent?

Who wants what you have to offer?

How much time, energy, and effort do you devote to each of the Pursuits?

Where Should You Go Next?

This is often the most difficult question of all. But it is easier to answer knowing that you are simply taking a next step, moving forward, not attached to a final destination or outcome.

Will you grow your relevance and your purpose if you continue to put the same amount of energy into a Pursuit? Even if you put less energy into a Pursuit? Only if you put more energy into a Pursuit?

What do you really want out of your life?

Your work?

Your relationships?

Yourself?

The answers to these questions will launch you on a unique journey among and through the Four Pursuits of Prosperity, Discovery, Connection, and Meaning. The Four Pursuits are the means to Relevant Purpose, and ultimately to the cultivation of *Zing*. They are the core inspirations for all that we choose to do, and the way we choose to do it. At the root of all our behavior, we are compelled to build capacity, acquire knowledge, interconnect with people, and help them to be relevant and purposeful. The Four Pursuits express how we invest our time, but more importantly, reveal how we can live our lives.

"Do not go where the path may lead,
go instead where there is no path and leave a trail."

Ralph Waldo Emerson

5

The Fourfold Path

*The Fourfold Path
is the path of human vitality,
the Way to Zing.*

You are leading a life of destiny.

More precisely, you are leading *your* life of destiny, finding and charting your unique path. How do you find that destiny? How do you discover who you really are? How do you know where you need to go next? How do you know what to do?

The Fourfold Path of awareness, alignment, action, and actualization is the Way to *Zing*. It is a guide for navigating among and through the Four Pursuits, directing you towards your Relevant Purpose. The Fourfold Path is more than a way of being. It is a way of doing—an energy path of human vitality.

When you travel the Fourfold Path, you will experience an awakening of your passions and purpose synchronized with the world around you. The Fourfold Path is both the origin and the destination of heightened awareness, conscious alignment, integrated action, and relevant, purposeful actualization.

On the Fourfold Path, you are aware of where you are and where you can go. You align who you are with what the world needs from you. You take action toward your unique Relevant Purpose, actualizing *Zing* through prosperity, discovery, connection, and meaning, uniting your inner life force with the external world.

Awareness is open-mindful thinking, feeling, and being, igniting possibilities for the alignment of prosperity, discovery, connection, and meaning.

Alignment is dynamic reflecting, prioritizing, and integrating relevant and purposeful actions in pursuit of prosperity, discovery, connection, and meaning.

Action is deliberate and determined investing of your time and energy to specific pathways among and through the Four Pursuits, actualizing Relevant Purpose.

Actualization is realizing a work/life that awakens you, integrating your true purposes and passions with external relevance and value.

On the Fourfold Path, your present and future are concurrent. Every single minute of your life offers you a gift—an opportunity to live in the moment and to reach towards your destiny. Today's awareness, alignments, actions, and actualizations are tomorrow's possibilities.

Actualization stimulates new thoughts, feelings, passions, and purposes, all of which expand awareness. Expanded awareness initiates and redirects priorities, provoking re-alignment. Re-alignment causes re-action, which generates new actions and sparks new actualization.

Traveling the Fourfold Path is both a sequential and simultaneous journey through the Pursuits, an enlightened odyssey of cause and effect, and effect and cause. *Zing* is not a destination to be found at the end of the Fourfold Path, but the energy of human vitality to be experienced along the Way.

"The soul should always stand ajar,
ready to welcome the ecstatic experience."

Emily Dickinson

Awareness

With a mind in the present and an eye on the future,
awareness broadens vision and sharpens focus,
offering infinite possibilities
of prosperity, discovery, connection, and meaning.

What really matters to you?

Why?

Awareness is the origin of a two-directional journey, a journey inside yourself, and out into the external world. Both directions lead you towards your Relevant Purpose.

Awareness is a deep exploration of the essential "you"— your fundamental values, ideas, feelings, and beliefs. As you understand yourself at your inner core, it becomes possible to lead a work/life path that fulfills and matters. Awareness empowers you to identify clearly the passionate energies that provoke you.

It is also a comprehensive survey of your present "location"—the circumstances in which you currently find yourself. As you broaden your understanding of what is happening to you and around you, you can take the steps to make any necessary course corrections, and to pursue new possibilities.

Awareness expands your peripheral vision, multiplying your options, allowing you to uncover previously hidden pathways to prosperity, discovery, connection, and meaning. As your senses intensify, you direct your work and your life with precision and patience, uncovering answers to the fundamental underlying questions of your work/life journey:

"Who are you?"

"Where are you?"

and ultimately,

"Where must you go?"

With *Zing* Compass in hand you have a simple yet profound view of your world. You become both observer and observed, awakening to your true self and the real world around you. You are observing what is most important and what truly matters, to you and to others.

Raising awareness is a continuous process—an ongoing, evolving look inward, not a quick glance in a mirror. It is also a constant, far-reaching look outward. Introspection feeds awareness, providing knowledge of your true purposes and passions, leading to self-discovery. Open-mindedness also feeds awareness, leaving you receptive to possibilities and prospects. By looking inside out and outside in, you start to see landmarks—signals that direct you towards which pathways to follow, which to approach with caution, and which to avoid altogether.

Awareness is the impetus for proactive change. By being mindful of who and where you are, you set the stage for becoming who you want to be. By critically exploring what you are doing now, you can be open to the possibilities you need to be doing next. Your awareness will flourish when you are not only open-minded, but also open-mindful.

As your awareness magnifies, you will change and grow, evolving beyond current passions and purposes while simultaneously creating new ones, moving yourself closer and closer to your Relevant Purpose. And as you edge closer to your Relevant Purpose, awareness no longer is a conscious act. It becomes part of who you are, opening the gateway to what really matters.

"When the spirit does not work with the hand,
there is no art."

Leonardo da Vinci

Alignment

When we travel in Alignment,
work and life are integrated and fulfilling,
growing out of who we are and who we need to be.

Our work/life becomes the set of pathways we choose because
they bring us closer to our Relevant Purpose.

Picture a world . . .

where everything you do helps satisfy your most essential needs, desires, and wants, and those of the people you care about;

where your work grows out of who you are deep inside;

where what you choose to do is valued by many;

where you can't tell the difference between work and life because your work is helping you achieve your life's dreams, and your life is helping you succeed in your career and profession.

This is a life lived in alignment.

When you are in alignment, all your activities are part of a unified and integrated quest toward your Relevant Purpose, not separate facets of your life. Any activity carries with it the opportunity to serve all the Pursuits.

Pathways converge when you no longer view your work and your life as a balancing act. The search for work/life balance constrains your thinking, creating perceptions of limits and scarcity. When seeking balance, time you spend in one area is time taken away from another. Work takes away from life or life takes away from work.

Time contracts when you divide it up. But when you align your work/life, time expands. Work/life alignment directs you to pathways of multiple Pursuits, creating more time. The more aligned you are, the more time you will have. More time, more possibilities, more vitality... more *Zing*.

On the Fourfold Path, a deep sense of who you are and where you are propels you forward toward Relevant Purpose, provoking the question, "Where do you want to go?" An aligned work/life is purposeful, spending time at places you want to be, joined by the people who are most important to you

"Where do you want to go?" has its roots in some of the most significant questions you have been asked throughout your life.

"What do you want to be when you grow up?"

"Where do you want to go to school?"

"What are you going to do for a living?"

"What are you going to do when you retire?"

"What are your goals in life?"

Answering these questions can often be vexing and frustrating because you are expected to know the "right" answer. Your answer is supposed to be conclusive, as if the question is an unresolved problem to be immediately and permanently settled. In reality, this reduces possibilities and closes off pathways.

Instead, "What do you want to be when you grow up?" is something you should be asking yourself every day. When traveling in alignment, you need only to decide where you are heading next, creating new possibilities and opening new pathways.

So, where do you want to go? What do you want to be when you grow up?

A good answer is "happy," for that is a choice you can make and is under your control.

A great answer is "relevant," but this is much harder for it is a choice with external validation.

The best answer is "me," for you are unique and special when you are who you are meant to be.

"The most effective way to do it, is to do it."

Amelia Earhart

Action

Zing is an active energy.
It pulls you and pushes you,
moving you and moving others.

If you want to prosper, you must act.

If you want to discover, you must act.

If you want to connect, you must act.

If you want to find meaning, you must act.

If you want your work/life to be more vital, you must act.

On the Fourfold Path, actions are thoughtful and conscious. *Zing* ignites when your aware and aligned inner passions and purposes manifest in relevant actions in the external world. You know why you are taking certain pathways and how you are going to take them. These pathways lead you closer towards your Relevant Purpose, generating more *Zing* and fueling further travel and adventure.

Taking action is a deliberate process, a sequence of activities moving you toward Relevant Purpose. Awareness of who you are and where you need to go creates focus, a prioritization of pathways among the Pursuits. Focus fuels commitment. Owning your decisions, you develop a plan for success and take the necessary steps to create results.

Following through and implementing with intention and intensity, you remain open-mindful to outcomes, making course corrections as you prosper, discover, connect, and find meaning.

Your actions are the foundation of your credibility— your representation to the world of who you are right now. But actions are more than just who you are today. They also establish who you will become. The actions you take today will actualize who you are in the future.

As you travel the Fourfold Path, do not be discouraged if your actions lead to unanticipated or undesired outcomes. You may take paths that are the long way, or even the wrong way. You may falter, trip, and fall. You may change course.

Keep going. Resiliency in your pursuit of prosperity, discovery, connection, and meaning will bring you closer to Relevant Purpose.

On the Fourfold Path, you are never overly disappointed with negative outcomes because you know things will change and/or you will change them. Sometimes, the most rewarding experiences in your work/life—the experiences that ultimately create the most *Zing*—are consequences of decisions that created challenges and difficulties. Traveling with awareness and alignment, and guided by Relevant

Purpose, you take action, embrace challenges, and persevere through them because you are progressing on your work/life journey.

Ultimately, taking action is not merely a decision about how you spend your time, but more importantly, how you invest it. Action is an exchange of time for current or future value. With awareness, in alignment, you decide how, when, where, and with whom to take action and invest time. When you invest in who you are, aligned with what the world needs from you, you create a promise of return on prosperity, discovery, connection, and meaning.

It is time for action.

What important actions will you take today?

"What you think, you become.
What you feel, you attract.
What you imagine, you create."

Gautama Buddha

Actualization

On the Fourfold Path,
the origins of today
create the destinies of tomorrow.

Actualization is the realization of your actions, your travels to and through the Four Pursuits. It manifests through the total experience of body, mind, heart, and soul—the perpetual awakening of your work/life journey toward Relevant Purpose. It shapes your realizations *of* experiences on the Fourfold Path, and your realizations *from* experiences.

Your experiences create prosperity, discovery, connection, and meaning. Your reflections on these experiences create new insights about yourself and the world, about your work/life. Actualization then creates new awareness, gives birth to new alignment possibilities, and directs you towards new actions of refined relevance and purpose in your work/life.

And so another awakening beckons.

Nothing is exactly as it seems until it is directly experienced. Experience surpasses planning, thinking, or intuiting because it is the consequence of actualization.

Experience tells you where you are, and where you need to go next. In experience, you hear the voice of who you are and who you may become.

This is bigger than learning from experiences; it is becoming those experiences and then taking them forward with you on the next stage of your work/life journey.

Actualization in its true essence is neither good nor bad, right nor wrong. Actualization just is. It is the pure voice of consequence, non-judgmental. It is your work/life speaking to you about how you are prospering, what you are discovering, with whom you are connecting, and why any of it matters.

Actualizations are way stations on the Fourfold Path. They are points of arrival, points of completion for recent paths traveled. They are also points of departure, the origins of future pathways and new destinies. They are work/life experiences that awaken new possibilities and new adventures. Actualizations create more awareness, focus alignment, and catalyze new actions in your personal Pursuits of Prosperity, Discovery, Connection, and Meaning.

What are you accomplishing today?

What are you learning?

Whom are you helping?

How are you making a difference?

Passage Two

A Venture of One

Each and every day of your life is a unique opportunity for adventure, full of possibilities to experience the extraordinary.

With mountains to climb, bridges to cross, and rivers to run, the Way of *Zing* guides you on that adventure, providing visibility and clarity across the landscapes of the world, and into yourself. Through the ongoing exploration of the Four Pursuits of Prosperity, Discovery, Connection, and Meaning, you are deliberately establishing calibration points—a "*Zing* Compass" for consciously directing your work/life journey in meaningful ways, towards all the things that matter. Navigating the Fourfold Path, you ignite inner purpose while building relevance with the world, energizing your unique life of human vitality.

But, while surveying the work/life landscape, you realize something significant. The world is changing, dramatically. Life is more complicated and accelerated, work increasingly migratory and ubiquitous. The well-worn tracks, trails and treks of traditional jobs and careers—historically the Holy Grail to lifelong fulfillment and success—have become paths of misdirection, leading to false hope, lost opportunities, and unrealized dreams. They simply do not look appealing or inviting. And they certainly won't take you where you want to go.

Profoundly awakened, you ponder.

How do I navigate this new world?
How do I apply the Way of *Zing* to this reality?
How do I chart a meaningful work/life adventure?

By living your work/life as a Venture of One.

Your Venture of One is the application of the Way of *Zing* to your work/life, the conscious synthesis of everything you are actualizing in your unique and personal journey. Your Venture encompasses the work you are doing and the intrinsic and extrinsic wealth you generate. It flourishes with the skills that you are learning, embraces the people you are meeting and cherishes the relationships you build. Ultimately, your Venture of One manifests in the impact you are having on the world.

As a Venture of One, you have an ultimate mission: Relevant Purpose. You want to matter. Relevance and purpose serve as reflection and origin points for charting pathways as you venture forward through work and life.

Your *Zing* Compass helps you assess and define each of the Pursuits, revealing pathways which invoke passion and inspire action. As you consider what prosperity, discovery, connection, and meaning signify to you, your mission begins to materialize. Individually and collectively, the Pursuits serve as reflection points for decision-making,

112

uncovering and identifying pathways for integrating work and life. You progress ahead, thoughtfully and consciously, making work/life choices to align purpose with relevance.

By formulating a work/life vision of who you really are, aligned with what the world really needs from you, you are empowered to become who you really need to be. You thoughtfully chart a strategic map of your journey among and through the Four Pursuits.

- Pursuing prosperity to build value and exchange with the world: to thrive.
- Pursuing discovery to nurture talents, expand knowledge, and evolve wisdom: to grow.
- Pursuing connection to build community, and cultivate deep and meaningful relationships: to give.
- Pursuing meaning to actualize what matters to you and to others: to serve.

Self-directed, success looks much different when living as a Venture of One. Successful Ventures are measured by a quadruple bottom line, each Pursuit offering perspective on your relevance and purpose. The Four Pursuits are a set of reference metrics to assess progress and make course corrections. Your quadruple bottom line grows when your inner energies align with external opportunities.

The Pursuits are dynamic as you change your life, and as life changes you. Things that you hold important today may become less important tomorrow. Things that are less important today may become extremely important tomorrow. When everything is mapped back to the Pursuits of Prosperity, Discovery, Connection, and Meaning, you gain clarity to act on the things that really matter.

Venturing forward, you travel pathways of external relevance and internal purpose, an aligned and integrated process where success is possible every single day—a process where the life of work and the work of life align, creating a work/life, igniting your unique energy of *Zing*.

Zing Pathways

You are **The Business of You**, *working for you, as you serve others.*

Your unique skills, talents, and experiences are the foundation of your **Most Valuable Asset**—*you.*

Entrepreneurial Pathfinding *anticipates change, dynamically aligning your Pursuits as you propel your work/life into motion.*

Risk Rewards, *because each risk taken creates experience, better preparing you for the next risk, building confidence while reducing fear.*

The University of You *is your own center of infinite learning, a mind state of personal evolution and development, a pathway which you travel for a lifetime.*

Learning your Way, *you learn how you learn best, building the skill to build skill, the talent to build talent, and the experience to build experience.*

Trying new things in new ways and new places,
Navigating Between Worlds *explores the unknown,*
expanding opportunities for relevance and purpose.

*The **Quest of Curiosity** dissatisfies curiosity, leading to*
new questions and opening paths to new discoveries.

*The **Caravan** is the people at the heart of your Venture, a*
unique community of shared intimacies and possibilities,
forged through your distinct power of connectivity.

*Traveling with **Trust**, you genuinely value the unique*
contributions of your companions, discovering their special
offerings while accepting their differences.

*The **Language of Zing** is a communication platform that*
categorizes, defines, and assesses the critical elements in a
work/life, promoting dialogue about what really matters.

The more you give, the more generous the world becomes,
*as the **Guide to Giving** inspires you to build value, so you can*
serve the world.

*Leading your Venture requires a strong **Personal***
***Charter**, a foundation of values, ideas, feelings, and beliefs*
that drive behavior and decision-making.

*Your work and life synchronize on **The Road Best Traveled,** choosing paths that integrate the Pursuits, leading to concurrent prosperity, discovery, connection, and meaning.*

*Sometimes the best path forward is traveled by being still, in a **Place of Refuge,** your harbor for refueling, replenishing, and revitalizing.*

*Making every moment matter, you are aware of all that is happening, seeing what must be done, doing what is necessary, **Leading the Way.***

1

The Business of You

A Venture of One is much more than a perspective on a job and career. It is the intentional integration of work and life directed towards relevance and purpose. As a Venture, work is an individually determined and selected set of activities focused on actualizing Relevant Purpose. Total compensation is the remuneration received as measured against the Four Pursuits, a quadruple bottom line.

By integrating work into life and life into work, you are navigating the pathways towards Relevant Purpose, building and growing vitality. More and more energized, you begin to direct your work/life with all the intensity, commitment, and efficiency of a dynamic organization. You are building a work/life business, and that business is you.

The Business of You is an ongoing enterprise to build and grow self-defined prosperity by creating value for others. It encompasses the exploration and identification of opportunities to provide relevant skills, discover and apply talent, connect with those who need what you offer, and deliver meaningful value. Supporting your integrated and aligned quest toward Relevant Purpose, the Business of You incorporates any activity you pursue to generate currency for exchange. The basis of that currency is relevance and value to others. When executed as part of an integrated work/life, all of the activities in which you purposively engage contribute to your quadruple bottom line.

As the leader of your Business, you will serve many, but you work for yourself—not another person, company, institution, or organization. You work for you. A Business of You liberates you from the emotional and mental shackles of working for others, while instilling the authority and responsibility to provide value to all those you serve.

Directing the Business of You may include taking on roles or assignments at a company or organization, or even working for multiple organizations simultaneously. These commitments will require the performance of certain tasks, producing specific deliverables, as you provide your unique skills and talents in service to clients, customers, patients, employees, managers, audiences, and communities. But no specific role completely defines you or your Venture. When you work for you, these paths have been deliberately chosen in service to your Relevant Purpose. You make your work/life; it does not make you.

As a Business of You, work roles and assignments are no longer viewed as permanent places of professional refuge. They are impermanent, serving as stepping stones for enhancing current and future relevance. Some will last longer than others, and some may be indefinite, but no specific role will last forever. When these assignments inevitably end, you will still be a self-sustaining enterprise working for you, traveling down the pathways of relevance and purpose.

This mind state transforms how we navigate and progress through our work lives. Typically, a traditional career is directed toward some distant long-term objective, an ultimate job title, position, and salary. The things that really matter are often deferred to a far-off time in the future, and a lot of vital energy is lost along the way. Accomplishment and success become ephemeral and fleeting when merely a means to an end.

In contrast, the Business of You operates in perpetual service to Relevant Purpose. Each and every day, your true work/life Venture manifests, liberating you from conventional career paths, job titles, and institutional labels. As a Venture of One, you have already reached the ultimate role, the leader of the Business of You.

2

Most Valuable Asset

As a Venture of One, you are your most valuable asset. Not the wealth you have accumulated, nor anything that you own.

The most important asset in your world is you. The unique skills, experiences, and talents that you have developed over the course of your lifetime are the foundation of that asset. Your specific prosperity, discoveries, connections, and meaning serve as personal capital to align and exchange with others, now and in the future. These Pursuits are your greatest source of treasure and lifelong currency, the resources you will use to travel the world on your work/life journey.

Your unique value is based upon your ongoing relevance. Relevance is a fluid valuation by others of your utility and worth, not a singular accomplishment earned or a permanent honor bestowed. It is the basis of your personal asset. Your asset grows with ongoing investment in Pursuits that have consequence for others. When your resources are relevant, people need what you have. They will trade with you. When your talents are relevant, people need what you know, and what you can do. They will hire you. When your connections are relevant, people want to be part of your network. They want to be with you. When you are relevant, your work/life makes a difference.

But you are more than the sum of your Pursuits. In totality, your prosperity, discoveries, connections, and meaning create your own unique work/life brand and help establish your brand equity. Your brand is your story, the tale of your Venture. It is more than a job title, resume, or degree. As part of your Venture of One, your brand is an adventure story, your quest for Relevant Purpose. It is a tale of unimaginable accomplishments and countless discoveries—a Venture that awakens to opportunity, discovers paths to capitalize on that opportunity, builds capacity to enhance value, and connects with those who need what you have.

Sometimes, your work, your identity, and even your life get defined by organizational job titles. Being characterized solely by a job title is limiting, narrow, inadequate, and incomplete. You are so much more than your job title. It just does not tell your whole story. And you certainly accomplish much more than what is in your job description. As a Venture of One, your personal brand is your own unique work/life story to tell, evolving and growing as your Pursuits change over time. You are the developer of your brand and the author of your story—a story that no one else can write.

Your brand is also your reputation. It is a story about you as told by other people, to other people. It is what others see in you, and say about you. Your brand features your individual competence and expertise—your core skills—as seen and needed by others. It underscores your special accomplishments and experiences, the inimitable adventures of your work/life journey. Your brand is why people want to exchange with the Business of You.

Your reputation creates advocates, people that help you with your Venture as you help them with theirs. This reciprocity is the foundation of credibility. Helping others successfully navigate their pathways demonstrates your relevance and establishes your credibility, for they are all building their Ventures.

Brand equity is founded in your unique ability to prosper and help others prosper, to discover and help others discover, to connect and help others connect, and to create meaning and help others create meaning.

Most importantly, your story is your opportunity to convey who you really are. Your story is what you do, and how others perceive it. It is the opportunity for others to see who you really are and to demonstrate what you truly value. It is the opportunity to unveil the authenticity of your Venture and your ability to deliver relevance with integrity. It demonstrates what is meaningful to you—what you value—in yourself and others.

What is your story?

3

Entrepreneurial Pathfinding

No one has ever walked in your shoes, and no one ever will.

Your unique work/life journey has taken you to many places, resulting in countless experiences. The decisions made, paths chosen, and the roads traveled have all led you to where you are today. The paths you choose today, lead you to who you are tomorrow.

Standing at the origin of new paths and new beginnings, you have choices regarding where to travel next—choices that direct you to your work/life destiny.

Rarely, if ever, is that direction an obvious straight and unobstructed path forward. Living in an age of accelerated change and mobility presents unique challenges. Work/life paths are often cloudy, chaotic, or congested, and not always easily identifiable or recognizable. Often, there are roadblocks to a clear and distinct path forward.

Therein lies the opportunity. By selecting and charting your own path, you are compelled to master the art of navigation. You become an entrepreneurial pathfinder, dynamically aligning your Pursuits in a climate of ever-present change.

Entrepreneurial pathfinding is the course of action for progressing forward on your Venture, putting your self-defined Pursuits into motion as you make work/life decisions. You are taking steps forward to become better, more vital. Making choices that continuously advance your work/life, proactively identifying new paths, and dynamically aligning those that you initiate and in which you participate. Proceeding with entrepreneurial intent, you see a world full of possibility for applying your existing skills, abilities, and experiences in new and different ways, and in new and different places. Anticipating changing trends and adapting accordingly, you begin to see opportunities that others may not, and develop new and distinct talents in preparation for the world of tomorrow.

Entrepreneurial pathfinding has you apply your energy towards the actions and activities that matter most. It is a choice to go where not only your work is valued, but where people are drawn to you, and your energy. You have the power to determine how you want to invest your time and energy, and with whom.

If you are a technologist, seek ways to generate additional revenue or reduce expenses for your company. Demonstrate for others the critical thinking skills that make you more than just a tech geek.

If you are a graphic artist, ensure you understand the unique needs of your client base by learning about their business and the customers they serve. Understand their supply chain and their market place.

If you are a medical provider, embrace the technological advances that are transforming your field. Proactively engage and collaborate with your technical and operational support teams.

If you are in financial services, seek ways to help propel the sales efforts of the organization. Show that you not only know how to crunch the numbers, but also what they mean and what course of action they might reveal.

If you are a teacher, seek new ways to apply what you know. Find special and unique ways to reach others, one student at a time.

If you are a leader, know when to follow, and know when to get out of the way. Regardless of your role, demonstrate your ability to lead yourself in creative and innovative ways.

As an entrepreneurial pathfinder, you need not be an entrepreneur, the founder of a new product or service. However, you are the founder of your Venture of One. To succeed in our dynamic, accelerating world, it is paramount that you embrace embracing entrepreneurial skills and behaviors. Your quadruple bottom line grows by building and practicing entrepreneurial skills that support your Pursuits—prioritizing to prosper, learning to discover, engaging to connect, and focusing to create meaning.

Prosperity gathers through the prioritization and allocation of capital resources—money, energy, and time—towards both immediate results and long-term investments. Discoveries advance from curiosity and an insatiable appetite for learning, building capacity, and transforming capabilities through questioning and acting upon what is and what can be. Connections multiply by the ability to create engagement, inspiring people to work with you, to invest in you, and to seek out what you have to offer. Meaning intensifies with purpose-driven focus, commitment, and the relentless pursuit of mission.

The synthesis of these particular skills makes you distinctive and unique. By embracing your entrepreneurial individuality, you will find that others respond to your authenticity, integrity, and competence. These characteristics travel well, for they are universal—relevant across multiple situations and environments. Entrepreneurial capacity is the talent that leaders are seeking, the set of skills that build long-term value, relevance, and independence.

Beyond these universal skills, successful entrepreneurial pathfinding is elevated by specialized expertise. To be known and acknowledged for a specific talent or skill set is to create a unique value proposition supporting your entrepreneurial story. Your personal asset is most valued by others when it encompasses a relevant expertise or technical proficiency coupled with desired entrepreneurial traits. This is particularly important early on in your work/life journey, as you launch your Venture. It gets you in the game, and serves as a mark of distinction as you move your Venture forward, building momentum, and broadening paths along the way.

Inherent in entrepreneurial pathfinding is action. However, taking action alone is not sufficient for your Venture to prosper. Recognizing there is a difference between activity and productivity, entrepreneurial pathfinding is focused on discovering paths that get things done. These actions include long-term investments and short-term sacrifices in service to your Relevant Purpose. However, in the relentless pursuit of your mission, you are not attached to a specific path, process, or outcome. You are attached to solving the problem and serving the need, not a preconceived solution. Your acts are not anchored by what was, but propelled by what is, and what can be. You celebrate both success and failure, using them as springboards for the future.

When you are entrepreneurially pathfinding, you have a keen awareness of the underlying attributes of the work/life activities in which you engage. You choose the aspects, qualities, and characteristics that makes them exciting, interesting, and fulfilling to you:

Are you driven by challenge, independence, collaboration, responsibility, security, companionship, diversity, familiarity, and/or significance in your work?

Do you like solving problems, leading people, identifying priorities, interacting with others, or creating efficiencies?

Do you want to work with your hands? Do you prefer physical activity?

Do you prefer self-starting activities, detail-oriented tasks, working in teams, or work that requires multi-tasking?

Do you like to be inside or outside, with others or alone, in front of a crowd or behind the scenes?

Are you driven to serve others?

Your *Zing* Compass is a pathfinding tool, helping you to explore attributes by framing the questions of why, how, and with whom you invest your time. As you seek out work and activities with the attributes most important to you, your internally felt experiences become connected with your external life.

What are the preferences you hold for the paths and pathways you travel?

Only when you answer this question will your *Zing* Compass point to where you should go next.

As your Venture progresses and prospers, you will find yourself increasingly independent and liberated, growing and evolving as your purposes and passions change. Liberation does not spring forth from hoarding wealth or from isolated self-sufficiency. It comes from your travels among the Pursuits as you accumulate and share prosperity, discovery, connection, and meaning, creating currency for future adventure and growth. This currency fuels an expansion of personal development and independence, an independence enabling you to be a sustainable, creative, and perpetually productive Venture.

Free from the shackles of institutions, your independence guides you to treasures in places you previously failed to look—inside yourself and out. Wisdom is born through the exhilaration of experience, and newly developed talents, skills, or knowledge. Love and intimacy are found through the formation of deep and meaningful relationships. Meaning deepens and proliferates as you apply your new Way to ponder the deeper questions in life in your personal quest for truth.

For an entrepreneurial pathfinder, prosperity takes on a newfound importance, becoming a different kind of treasure. Prosperity enables you to fully actualize the deep elements inside of you, creating currency to limitlessly travel the world, inside and out. Riches are not found at the end of the journey, but in the paths chosen along the Way.

4

Risk Rewards

You are confronted with short-term and long-term risks every day. Risk is inherent in any Venture you pursue, for the road ahead is unknown and the outcomes uncertain. Pathways chosen, paths traveled, and actions taken all carry varying levels of risk. Risk is a part of life, and as a Venture of One, risks are not avoided—they are enthusiastically embraced. Taking risks is a push forward, an invitation to participate and join in—to try. Risk is a catalyst for transformation, provoking entrepreneurial pathfinding, building your personal asset, growing the Business of You, and ultimately, for increasing your quadruple bottom line.

We live in an age of shifts, transitions, and fluctuations. As a Venture of One in a perpetually changing world, your progress is fueled by risk. Taking on new assignments and jumping into new activities, your Business adapts and grows in response to the risks taken. These new opportunities and adventures build your asset, growing capabilities and vitality as you prosper from successes and learn from mistakes made. Each risk taken opens up new paths, creating more choices and possibilities, and expediting your pathfinding. Risk is the adversary of the status quo. Your Venture will not progress by standing still.

Despite the opportunities made possible by risk, many times we have an innate resistance to taking risks. Risk has a negative association, frequently provoking internal unrest or anxiety. We feel that risk may expose us to danger and the possibility that something unwelcoming or unpleasant will happen. We believe that risk is difficult, for it will involve trial, tribulation and the need to change. We want to run from risk and hide from it.

At other times, we may approach risk with reckless abandon, with little thought to the consequences of our behavior. Risk is thrill, excitement, something that is actively pursued for its own sake. We move forward without care for ourselves or empathy for others. Engaging risk carelessly, we believe ourselves immune to negative outcomes. Or we just don't care. Seduced by the moment, we misunderstand or disregard the ramifications of our actions, foregoing long-term considerations for immediate reward.

Risk-taking is the active reconciler between danger, caution, and opportunity. Balancing hope and fear, optimism and pessimism, and confidence and doubt, the risks you take are a direct reflection of this reconciliation. Successful risk-takers are restless optimists. They are relentless in pursuit of improvement and progress, optimistic and confident that they will be better, stronger and more vital. But they are also prudent in their choices and vigilant in the execution of their actions.

Any worthy Venture engages in some risk, for often the biggest risk is to not take risks at all. When you play it safe, you do not initiate the adaptive measures necessary to create a perpetually relevant and purposeful Venture. Failure to take risks is one of the great inhibitors to progress and advancement in a work/life. When you take risks, you adventure into uncharted lands, learning vast and new things about yourself as you discover new frontiers. Each risk taken reveals a deeper understanding of your personal risk tolerance, and prepares you for the next steps in your life, and the next risk. This intimacy with risk builds further capacity for calculated, well-planned, and well-thought-out risk-taking, mitigating long-term risks. You begin to understand risk, both strategically and situationally.

Taking risks is a way to uncover paths of change, for you and for others. Risk awakens your Venture of One to opportunities for change, discovers paths to capitalize on those opportunities, building capacity and enhancing value. In today's reality, change will be part of your work/life journey, for even if you do not change, the world will. If you choose to avoid risk and fight change, you will head down a path to intrinsic and extrinsic bankrupcy, to work/life obsolescence. However, if you embrace risk and change, you will travel to new realms of prosperity, discovery, connection, and meaning. Enact change, adapt to change, follow change, and engage change. At the pinnacle, you can be change.

Serendipitously, embedded in the Fourfold Path is a risk-engagement process that accelerates your willingness and ability to manage risk while enacting change. Awareness provides information for a situational assessment of your capabilities and motivations, and of external opportunities and obstacles. You evaluate not just what you are able to do to progress on your Venture, but also what you are willing to do. Similarly, you scrutinize possibilities and perils, consciously aligning your talents, skills, and experience with opportunities that match your abilities and the attributes you most desire. With awareness, prospects for the Business of You expand, and threats of asset obsolescence are more easily detected.

When your intentions are actualized, risk is constructive, regardless of outcome. With each risk pursued, the more comfortable and skilled you become in risk taking, the better prepared and more excited you are for the next. Your analytical skills are honed, intuitions sharpened, and capabilities grown. The very act of engaging in conscious and active risk diminishes it. Repetition with risk breeds familiarity, confidence and skill, and the risk-engagement process becomes an integral part of the Business of You.

As you walk the Fourfold Path, there will be obstacles, challenges, and dangers to the most well-thought-out plan. Outcomes and expectations rarely actualize exactly as they are envisioned or intended, making risk-engagement an ongoing process. It requires adaptability and flexibility, and pivoting and path changes. Learning from challenges conquered and mistakes made, you step forward, and sometimes you misstep forward. Either way, the experience matters. Shifting your perspective of who you are and where you should go next, experience builds on experience, fine-tuning your *Zing* Compass.

With every risk that brings about new challenges and opportunities for relevance and purpose, your Venture of One becomes increasingly versatile. In the end, risk is not a choice, it is a reality. Stepping forward on the Fourfold Path, engaging risk fuels the energy necessary for your Venture to grow and prosper, progress and change, unite and connect, and find purpose and meaning. As you experience risk, you uncover paths to places you had never dreamed, creating adventures you had never dreamed possible. Your vital energy expands as risk becomes its own reward.

Calibrations

How are your most valuable talents & experiences relevant to others?

What are you doing to build new talents?

Are you passionate about your work? How can you make it more meaningful?

Are you spending time with the people you value and that value you?

5

The University of You

Your quest for Relevant Purpose is a search for answers to life's most important questions, discovering who you are, where you are now, and where you want and need to go next. Discovery is a unique and personal adventure, for only you can discover the real you. Only you can determine what matters the most to you, and how you can matter the most to others. Learning what you want to know, and what you need to know, you act on these discoveries, pursuing the paths of your Relevant Purpose. As a Venture of One, you are the center of your lifelong exploration and learning—a school for inspiring perpetual curiosity and expanding relevant knowledge and skills. You are the University of You.

The University of You is not a specific place, with ivory towers and hallowed halls. It is present anywhere there is an opportunity to discover. When you are traveling towards Relevant Purpose, opportunities to discover are everywhere. Every person you meet, every action you take, every performance you see, every gallery or museum you visit, every lecture you hear, every book you read, and every conference you attend are all part of your University's program. All the work you perform, the assignments you tackle, and the projects you take on are work-study programs at your University. The University of You may include time invested in school, as a student in seminars and courses. However, graduation is never the end of learning. Rather, it is the commencement of all there is to explore and learn.

As the University of You, you decide what you are going to learn, identifying key areas of focus, understanding the attributes that motivate you, and developing the skills you need to invest your time in the work/life activities that energize you. The curriculum preparing you for your Venture is intimate and evolving, as you learn to align your Pursuits and travel your Fourfold Path. Awareness of what you know and what you need to learn uncovers paths leading to future prosperity, discovery, connection, and meaning. If you lack prosperity, discover ways to earn it by exploring what others need and value. If you don't know what to learn, learn anything and discover what provokes and inspires you. If you lack connection, discover commonality in purpose, passion, or relevance. If you do not know what matters, find meaning in discovery, identifying new paths of Pursuit.

Not knowing often elicits feelings of anxiety, insecurity, and fear. This is even more pronounced when the unknown encompasses our core purposes, passions, and future directions. The University of You is a pathway which embraces the power of the unknown. Not knowing is the first step on a path of personal transformation and growth. The unknown leads to new experiences and new understandings, developing and applying the necessary skills and knowledge to accomplish your Venture's mission.

The University of You is the eyes and ears of opportunity, a mind state of personal evolution and development, and a pathway of ongoing relevance down which you travel for a lifetime. Applying your talents and experiences creates new ones, transforming capability into ability. This leads to a more vital life, generating *Zing*. Traveling from knowing to doing and from understanding to experiencing, you create unrelenting, incessant, continuous learning—infinite learning.

6

Learning your Way

The paths to learning are countless and dynamic, encompassing not only what and why you learn, but also how, where, when, and with whom you learn. Learning how to learn is the catalyst for infinite learning and the foundation for universal navigation and travel. When you know how to learn, you can go anywhere you want with confidence and efficacy.

Learning how to learn catalyzes personal transformation and growth, expanding pathways and uncovering paths, enabling you to develop other universal skills that are valuable to you and the world. It is the skill to build skill, the talent to build talent, the experience to build experience. It is a primary skill utilized to build vitality and to drive your Venture forward.

But learning to learn is more than building an asset. It is an asset itself, a highly desirable capability that you carry with you for a lifetime. When you have this asset, people notice. It speaks to your commitment and willingness to transform and change, and to become better and more vital.

It demonstrates the passion to do what is necessary. People will see this in you, and they will want it. Learning to learn becomes a part of your story, your distinct learning way.

Learning how to learn is a uniquely customized and specialized skill set, fine-tuned and honed over time. As this skill develops, you are increasingly competent in identifying paths where you learn best, and where you learn the most. Navigating through a myriad of learning environments, learning to learn unveils places of comfort, and areas where you will experience challenge.

Are you investing time in situations where your unique way of learning is actualized, creating an unquenchable thirst for discovery?

Learning your Way, the Fourfold Path directs your learning to the things that truly matter. Awareness reveals where you are most aligned in your Pursuits, and where there are knowledge and skill gaps. By prioritizing your learning and directing actions that actualize into relevant talents, skills and experiences, you expand your ability to learn in meaningful ways.

Like any other skill, learning to learn requires repetition and practice. It will take some work, and an investment of time and energy. Mastery comes through practice and commitment, a willingness to work hard, doing what is necessary to actualize relevance and purpose. The more you practice and learn, the more you realize how much there is yet still to learn. Your ability to build, grow, and sustain your Venture becomes both destination and journey. Infinite learning becomes a way of life, an energy that fuels prosperity, discovery, connection, and meaning—a life of *Zing.*

7

Navigating Between Worlds

The pursuit of Relevant Purpose is not a linear journey, a journey to a specific destiny. It is a journey to many places, traveled by navigating between worlds. Your *Zing* Compass rarely points in one direction. Frequently, it points in many directions, towards multiple Pursuits.

When you travel toward only a specific destiny, you can develop tunnel vision, becoming so focused on the destination that you miss opportunities, and people to engage along the way. Navigating between worlds entails seeking out new traveling experiences, building and growing relevance and purpose every step of the way. You will find new sources of success, new possibilities for growth, new friends with whom to connect, and new opportunities to make a difference.

Navigating between worlds means trying new things, in new ways, in new places. Your University is full of possibilities, and deep and insightful learning happens in unfamiliar locations by exploring the unknown. Navigating between worlds changes and transforms you. This not only creates new skills, but also reveals new passions and purposes, which lead to new interests. It builds your capacity to blaze new paths and unveil new Pursuits.

When work assignments offer skill building and learning opportunities, raise your hand and seize them. When your colleagues point to you as a go to resource for your existing skills, embrace the opportunities to engage with new and interesting team members.

Open-mindful "I can do this," replaces "I don't have time," and becomes a path to a new, improved, and better connected you—a more relevant and purposeful you.

This mind state may be integrated into your personal activities as well. Travel to new geographies, explore the cultures of the world, drive across the States, and visit the next town. Hike a new trail, bike a different route.

Navigating between worlds does not always necessitate traveling to new locations.

Pick up a guitar. Take a singing lesson. Buy a harmonica. Make music with your life.

Swing a racquet, hit a pitch, kick a ball, run a race, or swim a lap. Be in motion.

Paint, write, take pictures, race cars, build something, act out, or plant a garden.

Try new restaurants, new stores, new clothes, new movies, new books, and new music.

Meet new people. Make new friends.

Volunteer and help others. Serve food, greet people, offer talent, walk dogs, comfort the elderly, mentor youth, or coach a team. Do whatever provides intrinsic meaning while serving others, connecting you to a world greater than your own.

Surprise yourself. You have more potential than you think.

Venturing toward unchartered lands, discovering new realms, questioning everything and opening to infinite learning—this can be an intimidating and risky way to travel. Navigating between worlds teaches you to accept risk and embrace it. Each risk you undertake mitigates fear and propels you into worlds of opportunity and possibility. Inexperience becomes the genesis of new experiences and talents. Intimidation transforms into exhilaration and excitement. Fear becomes thrill.

Your University is a networked learning community of fellow travelers, constantly growing and developing as you share knowledge and support one another's learning. As you grow your learning community, include people who hold different ideas, the ones who disagree with you. Learning and knowledge often reside in between diversity of opinions, and at the intersection of divergent ideas.

When you navigate between worlds, search for teachers—knowledgeable experts whose deep expertise can help you answer questions, and more significantly, ask the right questions. Seek out mentors—guides to help you navigate through difficult life waters, and advisors that know what you do not. We can learn more about who we are when we see ourselves reflected through others.

Most important of all, search for students. To navigate successfully between worlds, you must simultaneously be a teacher and a student. If you want to learn something well, teach someone else about it. Teaching refines your understanding and your critical thinking, especially when the focus is more on how to help someone else learn and less on showing how much you know. As you organize ideas to facilitate someone else's learning, you develop new perspectives and deeper insights.

Zing multiples when you share your discoveries, and help others discover their own.

8

Quest of Curiosity

Admission to the University of You is not contingent upon test scores. Instead, it requires your relentless curiosity. Inquisitiveness sparks and sustains infinite learning. Curiosity is the foundation of your University, transforming you from passenger on your work/life journey into pathfinder and trailblazer. When you are curious, you uncover and identify pathways directed toward all Four Pursuits. These pathways are your University's coursework—the lessons you want to learn, and the lessons you need to learn. They are a quest of curiosity.

When you are pathfinding, your curiosity manifests as questions. The answers lead you closer towards your Relevant Purpose, simultaneously igniting new questions and fueling your curiosity. The art of questioning is a critical skill for a successful quest, for only through questions can you find the routes you must travel.

The greatest discoveries are born from asking, "What is?" and "What could be?" Directing "How can?" toward opportunities and problems uncovers prosperity, generating answers that create value and enhance relevance. Asking, "Who are you?" and "Who am I?" and listening with genuine interest as the answers lead toward empathy, understanding, commonality, and relationship fosters a strong connection. Questioning, "Why?" and "Why not?" uncovers meaning, encouraging critical and creative thinking.

Paradoxically, the quest of curiosity is not meant for satisfying it. The purpose of your quest is to dissatisfy curiosity. Question everything and you will discover that the more you learn, the more you want to learn, and the more curious you become. The answers that dissatisfy lead to new questions and open paths towards new discoveries. Be open to learning anything, but be especially mindful of those learning opportunities that provide the knowledge, tools, and skills to progress as a Venture of One. *Zing* gathers where curiosity is channeled toward, and aligned with, Relevant Purpose. Seek out expertise that is meaningful to you and that has value to others. You will know if you are asking the right questions when the answers provoke more curiosity.

The quest of curiosity takes you beyond asking questions. It is a call to action, igniting your passions and creating new ones. Curiosity inspires you to dig deeper, move faster, and try harder. It is relentless, fueling the pursuit of the Pursuits, moving you beyond learning to learn, and towards loving to learn.

Mark Gregory Nelson & Dr. William S. Silver

Calibrations

What do you need to learn to be more relevant and purposeful?

What do you want to learn about?

How can you help others learn to be more vital and fulfilled?

Who can teach you what you want and need to know?

9

The Caravan

You will not travel alone. You need others, and they need you.

Your Venture of One is interconnected, united by those with whom you exchange and prosper, learn and discover, love and connect, and share inspiration and meaning. Open-mindful to the diversity that strengthens joined Ventures, you recognize that commonality subordinates difference when there is shared purpose.

You possess a distinct power of connectivity. Others may know the same people, but no one else develops and maintains the same special connections and confidences. By interacting with colleagues, clients, friends, and family, and often engaging with people whom you have never met before, you are forging a unique connection of shared intimacies and possibilities. This is more than a business or social network. This is more than a community. It is your traveling Caravan, the people at the heart of your Venture.

Your Caravan is the unique set of personal and professional relationships you actualize on your work/life journey. A compilation of the partnerships you form, affiliations you make, friendships you build, and bonds that you forge. Evolving and dynamic, always in motion, your Caravan gathers momentum through the purposeful choice of traveling companions, and from chance encounters. Your Relevant Purpose becomes a rallying cry, a focus for building interconnected shared missions. People you seek out will answer the call. Sometimes those you did not look for will answer the call. As your Caravan expands and evolves, so do your capabilities, possibilities, and opportunities.

Work/life is more fulfilling when experienced with others. There is power in shared pursuit, shared action, and shared experience. Joined Ventures benefit from actualizations created together. You can take on more, accomplish more, and matter more. Life is not meant to be lived in isolation. There are people here to help you, and your Venture thrives in their company. Every person is a Venture of One, their own unique synthesis of diverse attributes and experiences. But individuality thirsts for expression, and that thirst may be quenched through the cup of community.

A Caravan is more than merely meeting and knowing people. It is actively built, aligned, and nurtured by genuinely valuing their purpose and relevance. Your traveling companions need you as much as you need them. They, too, want to be vital, creating possibilities of shared prosperity, discovery, connection, and meaning. Shared Pursuits and shared stories based on mutual respect, commitment, understanding, and empathy. Your Caravan is not an assembly of accumulation, but instead a gathering of giving. Flourishing through the shared mind state of perpetual service, it is built to help others help themselves, and in turn, help others help others.

Your Caravan is not built by making more connections, but by making the right connections. It is a purposeful gathering of Ventures, the shared lessons and experiences accumulated along your work/life journey. Seeking alignment and taking action, you choose where you are going and with whom you travel, so you are traveling with trust.

10

Traveling with Trust

Trust is the foundation of your Caravan, an asset that is built through interaction and exchange. Doing business together. Learning together. Laughing and caring together. Dreaming together. Devoting time to shared Pursuits. By sharing resources, you trust you will create more. By sharing knowledge, you trust you will learn. By sharing yourself with others, you trust they will share themselves with you. By sharing your heartfelt dreams with others, they will share theirs. Experiencing together is an act of trust, an investment of time that actualizes more trust in return.

Trust develops from the shared intimacy born of time-tested relationships. Relational, not transactional, your Caravan thrives and prospers through participation and engagement. The deals you cut, the agreements you make, and the bargains you reach all grow with relationships, but are not the ultimate objective. Exchanges are building blocks, the means for deepening relationships and reinforcing the integrity of your Caravan, individually and collectively. Transactions that do not support the wellness of a long-term sustainable relationship are foregone.

Opportunities to build trust manifest themselves daily. Look for someone who is struggling with a project, problem, or challenge, and offer unconditional assistance. Be of service to your Caravan.

Help a friend propel their Venture forward by using your specific expertise to bridge a knowledge, talent, or experience gap. Equip them, guide them, and make them better.

Learn about the talents and capabilities of the people in your Caravan, and connect those that can be of value to one another. Connecting people with solutions to people in need demonstrates your trust, and in turn, that they can trust you. People want to be sought after, love to be needed, and strive to be relevant.

Do the little things that are universally meaningful. Be kind, respectful, punctual, fair, honest, loyal, friendly, and genuine. Demonstrate who you are through the authenticity of your Venture. Show those in your Caravan the things you value most by the actions you take.

With time, bonds of trust will strengthen through shared acts and adventures. Trust is specific, and the measures of trust are varied. To grow trust, seek opportunities to value the unique contributions of your traveling companions. Discover their special offerings. Which extraordinary talents and skills do they bring to the Caravan? Do they bring focus, organization, drive, enthusiasm, analysis, creativity, versatility, discipline, and/or loyalty? What are their unique gifts?

Ask not merely whom you can trust, but what it is about them that fosters that trust, revealing pathways of alignment and compatibility. When relationships are purposeful, trust builds through the thoughtful investments of time, energy, and emotion.

Trust expands through passion for a common purpose, and the acceptance of difference. A true mark of trust is believing in people who are not like you. The basis of this trust is authenticity, where actions are consistent and in alignment with purported values, beliefs, and motivations, even when they are different from yours. When someone walks their talk, you can know who they are. When there is authenticity in action, you can acknowledge and accept diversity, creating a more powerful team. You each trust you will act in honor of common purpose, doing the right thing, in the right way—being there for each other and having one another's backs.

Traveling together, exploring commonalities and differences, successes will be achieved and mistakes will be made. Encourage progress by celebrating successes and failures, learning from both. Demonstrate your trust by counting on others. Trust that they will learn and grow in honor of their discoveries. Be a guide and supporter, not a critic and judge. Respect their willingness to both take on challenges and be challenged. Inspire action, seeking ways to align missions and actualize more relevance and more purpose.

The tension between individuality and community will lead to an organic evolution of your Caravan. Traveling companions will naturally depart, temporarily or permanently, when their Pursuits diverge. The ability for other travelers to choose to be part of your Caravan, or not, becomes a fabric of trust. Sometimes, you will be the one to initiate a departure of ways. This, too, is bound in trust. Trust that choosing separate paths is not a repudiation of a person, but a way to honor their unique Relevant Purpose while staying true to your own.

Your *Zing* Compass not only helps you assess how to invest your time, but also with whom. It serves as a barometer of trust testing the boundaries of behavior.

Who is important to your Venture? How?
With whom do you want to travel? Why?
Who adds to your energy? Who drains it?
Do you know who they really are?
Do they know the real you?

Choose your traveling companions wisely, assessing alignment, because in travel, we must trust.

11

Language of *Zing*

Over time, the Way of *Zing* evolves into more than a work/life philosophy and decision-making guide. It becomes its own language. Through a common body of words and symbols, it provides the means for discourse to help you and others lead a more vital and fulfilling life. A communication system of exchange, revelation, intimacy, and culture, it facilitates connection to the energy inside you and others. It becomes a language of human vitality, the language of *Zing*.

The language of *Zing* is an interactive platform that allows you to get to the heart of what matters. A vehicle to categorize, define and assess the elements in a work/life, this language initiates and promotes dialogue about the things that are truly important. The Pursuits are words and symbols for the elements in life, and when consistently used and applied through interchange, they become a vital component to work/life direction and guidance. Dialogue and connection with others deepens, and paths and pathways to and through the Four Pursuits expand. You gain clarity.

The framework of the *Zing* Compass directs the dialogue in a conscious and meaningful way by pointing to the quadrants and categorizing the elements of work/life. It is a systematic tool for exploration and assessment, guiding you to ask relevant and purposeful questions to dig deep inside yourself and others. With a common language, you can identify and understand the attributes of individuals that motivate and energize them, facilitating the understanding of values, ideas, feelings, and beliefs in a consistent and structured way.

Each of the Pursuits has its own inherent definition and dialect. Directing conversations to what is needed for Ventures to progress, prosperity becomes the voice of exchange. Financial accumulation and independence are part of the exchange, but you begin to notice that prosperity is much richer than material wealth. It broadens, encompassing knowledge, love, skills, health, connections, experience, spirituality, meaning, and wisdom. Exchange becomes much more than a discussion regarding transactions to make money. It evolves into a cooperative sharing of needs and values, uncovering ways to join in pursuit of relevance and purpose. Prosperity becomes defined through mutual success—winning with someone, not at the expense of someone.

The dialogue of discovery uncovers what has been learned, and reveals what is jointly understood. A shared framework, it becomes a way of growing together. The intimate conversations about personal experiences, trials, and challenges, successes and celebrations are important sources of work/life development. Many "ah ha" moments come during these dialogues as a long-hidden path suddenly becomes clear, because someone has given you clear directions that you are now able to follow.

The language of *Zing* creates intimacy through empathy. By becoming more connected to yourself, you gain insights into others. Self-discovery becomes human discovery, understandings you can apply to all those with whom you connect. You recognize what provokes others, and their preferences for communication and interchange. You are acutely conscious of your actions, and of theirs. Language becomes more than mere words and symbols when it is the thoughtful expression of mind, body, and spirit. In an effort to open the hearts and minds of others, you pick and choose your words wisely and monitor your actions carefully. You find significance in silence, a warm embrace, a subtle smile, or the soft touch of a hand. You begin to understand the shift of a body, the blink of an eye, the nod in approval, the drop of a face, the loss of attention, and the rigid response. When we speak of connection, we speak of not only what someone says, but also what we deeply understand.

Sharing meaning is culture created, one of the tools that brings communities together. Culture is commonality amongst diversity, where what we do together is bigger than what we do alone. When we share meaning, we are bonded in values, beliefs, and motivations. We are in connection across places, distance, and time; a community strengthened, a Caravan of trust, and a trusted Caravan.

The Fourfold Path is a methodology for building and sharing a common language, expediting your mission, and that of others. Communication and collaboration builds the trust that binds Ventures together. Awareness unveils elements of prosperity, discovery, connection, and meaning that are of consequence to others, creating understanding, empathy and intimacy. Alignment creates opportunities for partnership and cooperative path-taking. Action unleashes the power of teams, working and living together to leverage capabilities and actualize result. Sharing experiences strengthens connections, generating new opportunities for shared journeys.

Your personal perceptions create unique views of the world as you experience work/life through filters developed over time. When you focus your awareness and attention toward others' Pursuits, you build shared and new perceptions, seeing life through each other's eyes. Your awareness expands as you see through multiple lenses. Shared awareness directs and sharpens focus and sparks creativity, revealing new paths and pathways.

Alignment establishes shared priorities and shared Pursuits. Synchronizing common interests and passions synthesizes effort. Integrating diverse interests and passions leverages difference, strengthening and expanding the whole. In alignment, Ventures converge in shared mission, creating shared maps of future action.

Action is teamwork in motion, when joined Ventures are directed towards united Relevant Purpose. Working together creates exponential result by sharing ideas, experiences, and talents. Aligned action leverages time, energy, and resources. Success is a consequence of communicating priorities and plans, and collaborating on preparation and execution. Action unleashes a collective energy and effort, sparking synergy.

When joined Ventures actualize through result, momentum builds, creating opportunities for future paths and pathways of shared travel. Actualization creates the language of shared experience, realization, and appreciation. It initiates stories of adventures traveled together, obstacles overcome, and success achieved. But more than opportunities and stories, actualization creates bonds—bonds built on trust, knowledge, capability, care, admiration, experience, and appreciation. These bonds ignite the willful power to actualize tomorrow, together.

As you venture together in your Caravan, individual gratefulness empowers collective greatness, and you begin to understand. Where you travel is important, but traveling together makes the journey all the more worthwhile.

12

Guide to Giving

The energy of *Zing* resides inside each and every one of us. Wherever you travel, you carry deep within you the vital energy of who you really are. It may be activated in many ways, but none is more powerful than the giving of your authentic self. When your unique vitality is shared, you induce others to do the same. A source of inspiration, you are the catalyst for the exponential expansion of human vitality.

By giving, you provoke the world of others. A world where affluence provokes distribution, experience and knowledge provokes conveyance, skills, and talents provoke application, community provokes collaborative action, and meaning provokes collective impact. This ultimately provokes a world where value is not determined by how much you have, but by how much you give.

The Pursuit of Prosperity, Discovery, Connection, and Meaning is a work/life journey of giving, not getting. Sharing with others, not having, holding, or hoarding for yourself, giving is the offering of all you are to the world.

Your unique gifts are a call to action and responsibility to share your wealth, knowledge, connections, and beliefs for the benefit of others.

In pursuit of *Zing*, giving and sharing becomes a virtuous cycle of infinite possibility. You pursue prosperity, discovery, connection, and meaning to help others pursue their own prosperity, discovery, connection, and meaning. In turn, they will do the same.

The *Zing* Compass is a tool for giving, a way to assess and identify the needs of others and point them in the right direction. A collaboration tool and a leadership tool, a mentoring tool and a friendship tool, it is also a tool for asking the right questions. How am I helping others find prosperity, discovery, connection, and meaning? How will I guide others on their Way, helping them understand and appreciate who they really are, and who they need to be?

Traveling in a Caravan, the Fourfold Path serves as the guide to giving. Asking "What do I have to offer?" and "How can I be of service?" facilitates expanded and focused awareness. As you consider what you have to share and what you should share, giving becomes a unique balance of unfettered generosity and strategic application. Giving liberally creates new possibilities, for yourself and for others. Giving prudently, with thoughtfulness, discipline, and intentionality, creates alignment, serving your lifetime quest for Relevant Purpose.

Giving is a balanced and disciplined state of mind. If you give part of yourself today, how does it affect your ability to give tomorrow? Getting, holding, and having in isolation leads to missed opportunity and stagnation. It becomes self-limiting. Undisciplined and unrestrained giving will set you off course, leading to imbalance and future difficulty. Problems often result when you give something you do not have, or more importantly when you give what you are not. Opportunities proliferate when you practice aligned giving, when your relevance and purpose is consciously synchronized with the relevance and purpose of others.

Giving is a form of action. It is the active sharing of currencies, actualizing more giving in return. Generously sharing your material wealth and resources serves as an investment in your Relevant Purpose, and that of others, so they can share their prosperity. Giving your knowledge and wisdom helps others grow and prosper, especially when what you help them learn helps others learn. But often the most powerful currencies to give away are not tangible. They spring forth from connection and meaning. Notice the power of a smile. The energy activated by authentically asking, "How are you doing today?" and, "What do you think?" The vitality created when you show someone that you care.

Giving is a mind state of service and responsibility that permeates throughout your Caravan. Giving attracts others, initiating and creating shared value through shared mission. When you give, you demonstrate your value, and what you value. Giving resounds, becoming something that you do for others, with others. In connection, giving together joins assets to build assets, creating foundations of responsibility, and sharing your Caravan with those in need.

As you venture forward, you will find that the world is the great reciprocator. When you work hard at being a good person, good people will follow you. When you do the right thing, the right things ultimately happen to you. When you confide, you will gain confidants. When you are a companion, you will find companionship. When you share wisdom, you will gather wisdom in return. When you serve others, you will be served. The harder you work at giving who you are and what you have, the more generous the world becomes. The more you give, the greater the intrinsic and extrinsic returns. Your giving propels you forward, traveling further through the Way of *Zing*.

Calibrations

Whom will you help prosper?

Whom can you mentor to be a mentor?

Whom will you help make a difference?

How are you building a caravan of collective purpose?

13

Personal Charter

Your Venture of One has a mission: Relevant Purpose.

Leading your Venture requires a strong foundation of values, ideas, feelings, and beliefs that drive behavior and decision-making. This is your personal Charter, the integration of the "you" inside of you with the experiences accumulated along your work/life adventure. It is the essential you, the who you are at your core being. Your Charter represents the principles of your life, your universal truths. It is your point of view, your perspective on how the world works, and it serves as a guide to Relevant Purpose.

Your work/life journey offers a multitude of opportunities to prosper, discover, connect, and create meaning. When your Charter is translated into the language of *Zing*, it calibrates your *Zing* Compass, clarifying which aspects of each Pursuit are meaningful. What types of prosperity do you value? What ideas have been provoked by discovery? How do you feel about the people in your

Caravan? Do you truly believe in the choices you are making?

Over time, your Charter will be tested and examined. With new internal and external experiences, it will be appropriately modified. As you prosper, discover, and connect, you will reinforce vital components of your Charter, and dispel others, evolving meaning. Experiencing, questioning, and reflecting all strengthen your Charter, enabling you to modify or remove incompatible elements, and add new relevant ones. The more exploring you do and the more adventures you have, the more solid your Charter becomes. Your Charter clarifies choices, heightening your awareness and offering possibilities of dynamic alignment. It will inspire you to take specific actions, directing you towards paths you should follow and those to avoid, creating actualizations that matter.

In work/life, the hardest decisions often involve conflict of values, ideas, feelings, and beliefs—situations when you must make a choice between competing and equally compelling priorities. A strong Charter develops your ability to make decisions in these uncertain and difficult circumstances, helping find the opportunity in challenge and the solution in problems. It enables you to choose among options, and to discover new ones. It is a vehicle of possibility—of exploring and seeing beyond perceived limitations. Which options best align with your core purposes? Which choice has more relevance for others? Which actions must you take?

As you become more intimate with your Charter, your *Zing* Compass becomes more than a simple decision-making tool. It manifests as part of who you are, serving as an internal guide for all of work/life's decisions, big and small. You no longer consciously need to activate your *Zing* Compass for every decision, as it becomes a reflexive and subconscious capability, an innate process directing your work and life towards the things that matter.

Fully evolved, your Charter is more than a set of guidelines to follow. It is the foundation of your unique passions, the inspirational energy source for your Venture. Your personal Charter ignites the energy inside of you, transforming passions into actions and driving you towards Relevant Purpose. Galvanizing desire and focusing effort, your Charter inspires you to make a difference.

14

The Road Best Traveled

The road best traveled is an individually determined set of choices that put your values, ideas, feelings, and beliefs into action. It is the Fourfold Path actualized by you, in your Way. A unique path, it is your personal Charter in motion, directing you towards Relevant Purpose. You get to choose who you want to be and where you want to go next. You get to choose the road best traveled.

How do you make the choices that propel your Venture forward, and the choices that matter the most? By choosing paths that lead to concurrent prosperity, discovery, connection, and meaning.

Your *Zing* Compass guides you on the road best traveled by helping you identify pathways and paths that integrate the Pursuits. Your work and life synchronize when you travel paths of simultaneous Pursuit—when your body, mind, heart, and soul completely engage in work/life. This synchronization unites passion, purpose, and relevance.

Each element of the Fourfold Path can be enlisted to support choices of simultaneous Pursuit. Through awareness, alignment, action, and actualization, you can integrate existing paths or discover new ones. You know that you are on the road best traveled when the Pursuits converge into one path, actualizing all Pursuits together. The road best traveled is not found in a specific place. No one can tell you where it is and how to get there. You create the road best traveled through choices that integrate Pursuits, passions, relevance, and purpose.

As you travel on your work/life journey—growing prosperity, making discoveries, building connections, and evolving meaning—you recognize that your Venture of One has a deeper responsibility. The road best traveled holds an inherent commitment to the greater good. Being true to who you are and aligning it with what the world needs, you are acting on behalf of others in honor of a higher calling.

More than doing your best, the road best traveled is doing the best thing the best way, and for the greatest good. It is bigger than you. It is not enough to live up to your potential when you can help others live up to theirs. It is not enough to do your best when you can be your best. On the road best traveled, you are your best by helping others be their best. Your deeper responsibility is to empower others by helping them align who they are with what the world needs from them.

Empowerment is a catalyst for *Zing*, helping people to be more vital, to learn and grow, to be more interconnected, and more meaningful so that they, in turn, may serve others, generating more prosperity, more discovery, more connection, and more meaning. Empowerment is evolutionary improvement, making life better for the next person so that they, too, can make life better for the next person, and then the next community, and then next generation. Empowerment creates meaning for others, providing opportunity for them to help themselves and empower more people, creating more *Zing*.

By pursuing paths that matter to you, and matter to the others, serving selflessly and relentlessly, your Venture of One makes the world a better place. When actions are in alignment with a greater good, you are making a difference today while building for tomorrow.

15

Places of Refuge

Your Venture of One is primarily action oriented, taking you down paths of relevance and purpose. It is a relentless pursuit of the things that are meaningful, and that matter. However, meaning is not created solely through the actions of your work/life journey, but is also deeply experienced in places of refuge.

Your place of refuge is your harbor for refueling, replenishing, and revitalizing. It's a place where you relax and find peace, where your body calms, mind slows, heart warms, and soul revels. It is your place to rejoice and reflect, and where you can find inspiration, motivation, and encouragement.

It is where you go to celebrate your Venture's victories and accomplishments, a place of reward and recognition of a job well done. It's a gathering of the people who matter most, convening in celebration of success and achievement. It is also a place of solitude, basking in a moment of self-reflective gratitude and appreciation.

A safe-haven, your place of refuge offers comfort during times of difficulty. It is the place that gives you comfort during chaos, optimism during suffering, and hope when there is challenge. It's a place that helps make sense of the world when the world makes no sense, a place to find acceptance by others and embrace acceptance of yourself. It is a place to go when you feel you have done your best, and want to be better.

Your place of refuge is not limited by location, as it is a way of being and doing. It is something that you carry with you wherever you may go. Places of refuge know no boundaries; they are limitless and timeless.

A place of refuge may be found in a book and a glass of wine, or in the anonymity of strangers at a coffee shop, library, or park—enjoying, relaxing, recharging.

It's at a place of tranquility, like a church or a temple or a mosque or a sweat lodge or a shrine—sitting, praying, meditating, listening, being.

It's with family and neighbors and colleagues and teammates, or a night out with friends—connecting, caring, sharing, loving, laughing.

Sometimes refuge is found in activity—on a walk, run, or stroll. On a bike, on a court, on the slopes, on a course, on a river, in the woods. Driving, sailing, riding, flying, paddling, cycling, swimming, running, throwing, hitting, kicking, passing, playing.

Or in a hobby—building, fixing, gardening, cleaning, creating, making, solving.

It may be found in expression—singing, dancing, strumming, jamming, writing, drawing, painting.

In your place of refuge, your mind quiets as you begin to truly understand and appreciate who you are. Then, something magical can happen. You are more vital. You have more energy. You see more clearly. You understand more deeply. You appreciate more sincerely.

The workings of the world take on a whole new meaning—a meaning that was completely out of sight, out of reach. Trees look different, the sky looks different, and a ray of light on a river or behind a mountaintop looks different. Your vision becomes more acute and razor sharp. Your awareness becomes a whole-body experience. You can feel the energy of life and the interconnectivity of the universe, allowing you to fully experience the now, while charting a course for your future. This clarity and awareness creates comfort and confidence and guidance. It allows you to begin connecting the pathways between your inner purpose and your external realities. You don't see your *Zing* Compass; you feel it.

Often, we get so busy executing our lives, we are consumed by them. We don't take the time to pause, examine, and reflect. To appreciate, to understand, and to recognize. We are moving so swiftly to get to a destination, we forget why we are going there, or we don't know why we are going there in the first place. Sometimes the best path forward is being still.

We all have many places of refuge if we invest the time to go there.

16

Leading the Way

The Way of *Zing* is not merely a guide you follow; it is a life you lead. You are the leader of your life—always, and in all ways.

As a Venture of One, you lead the Business of You towards relevance and prosperity, liberating you from the boundaries of the traditional, unshackling the handcuffs of the institutional. You lead the University of You with incessant curiosity and discovery, ensuring readiness, equipping yourself with the knowledge and skills to face the challenges and opportunities of tomorrow. You lead your Caravan with trust, building connections, aligning Ventures, integrating experiences, and walking together down the road best traveled.

With leadership comes great authority and power, and also great responsibility—power and responsibility to manifest your values, ideas, feelings, and beliefs into relevance and purpose. The things you value, the ideas you create, the feelings you have, and beliefs you hold dear are unique and special. They are yours to lead, and to lead with. Only you can decide how to manifest your Charter into Pursuits, and choose the paths and pathways to your Relevant Purpose. Leading the Way, this responsibility is neither a weight to be carried nor a burden to bear. It is the motivational element of vital energy, the power to actualize meaning. The more responsibility you accept, the more meaning you can create, the more *Zing* you actualize. Leading the Way brings your energy to life.

The Fourfold Path is a Way to lead yourself and others, actualizing Pursuits that matter to you, and matter to the world. Through awareness, alignment, action, and actualization, your work and life synchronize as you travel pathways of simultaneous Pursuit. Your body, mind, heart, and soul completely engage in work/life, effortlessly sharing your life's work with the world. You are in the moment, uniting passion, purpose, and relevance, connecting with everything that is larger than you, creating meaning. Leading the Way, you are making a difference in the places you work, and in the communities where you live. You are making the world a better place.

You can make every moment matter. Every experience tells a story. When you are open-mindful and aware of all that is happening, you see what is necessary, doing what must be done. You can touch the hearts and souls of others, aligning their passions, purposes, and relevance with your own, creating collective purpose. Together, you are inspired to act on behalf of the greatest good. Inspirations become reality, actualizing inner energies into external realities, igniting *Zing*.

Your journey through work/life builds your relevance and value, a distinctive and exceptional offering to the world. People want what you have and your prosperity grows. You discover, and your capabilities and knowledge expand. You connect, and the un-manifested becomes manifested. You are prospering to build, discovering to understand, connecting to share, and creating meaningful ways to serve.

As you venture forward, making incomparable contributions to the world, you discover something very special.

The world needs not what you have, but who you really are.

Calibrations

What are your core values?

What ideas provoke and inspire you?

What do you believe really matters?

With whom do you share passions and purposes?

The End (of the Beginning)

Surveying the landscape of your work and life, Zing Compass in hand, you stand confidently, staring at the Fourfold Path ahead of you.

As you gaze into lands of Prosperity, Discovery, Connection, and Meaning, you pause and reflect on all of the adventures that led you to where you stand today. You reflect on battles won and battles lost, relationships built and relationships soured, experiences embraced and experiences discarded, and wealth accumulated and wealth squandered.

Calmly gazing out into the distance, you take a deep breath, and a voice affectionately whispers. "It is all going to be okay. You know the Way."

You begin to walk forward. In some new and strange way, your life is beginning to make sense; you are beginning to understand. Through the deep reflection of your past, while awakened to the present, the path forward is becoming increasingly clear. Somehow, some way, all of the opportunities taken and missed, challenges faced and avoided, and choices made for better or worse, provide clarity. No longer a weight to be carried, these experiences serve as points of light on the path forward. They offer guidance, direction, support, and energy.

You realize that you are different than you were. Way different. The passionate energy inside is ignited; the energy of others is more evident. You see and hear things you never noticed, and begin to understand what really matters to you and others. And you know why.

You are traveling the Way of Zing.

You are a Venture of One, with a mission of Relevant Purpose. You are on a work/life journey down the Fourfold Path, to the destiny of who you really are, synthesized with what the world needs. Your Venture is the origin and destination of enhanced awareness, conscious alignment, and meaningful action, actualizing your unique energy of human vitality.

Your Zing Compass leads you to the things that truly matter, directing you towards all you pursue. The Four Pursuits of Prosperity, Discovery, Connection, and Meaning not only guide you; they help define what matters to you. The Fourfold Path becomes a conscious process for making relevant, purposeful, and interconnected work and life decisions. Over time, this becomes less conscious, and then subconscious, as the Four Pursuits and the Fourfold Path become part of who you are.

As you experience the energy of vitality, you are awakened. Your inner passions and purposes evolve, changing how you see yourself, and how you view the world. This inner (r)evolution is transforming who you are and what you can do. Where you once saw challenge, you now seize opportunity. Where you once saw problems, you now create solutions. You perceive little things that used to seem small, but now really matter. You realize things that used to be a big deal don't really matter at all. Amazingly, you find that the very things that used to immobilize you, the things that created fear or pain, are the very things you cannot live without. You choose to do things you never would have done before you found the Way.

These changes are affecting the paths you take, and why you take them. Your steps are becoming increasingly deliberate, yet you glide with lightness, your feet ready to shift when unforeseen obstacles stand before you. Your curiosity drives you to your next exhilarating experience, your next new adventure, and your next newfound passion and purpose, allowing you to fully explore yourself and the world. You progress forward with a relentless intensity, open-mindful to different outcomes and alternate paths. You are putting your energy into action, actualizing experiences that will guide you on the next step forward toward Relevant Purpose.

And, as your work/life journey unfolds, taking you deeper and deeper on the Fourfold Path, you find yourself walking with destiny—the destiny of all that matters.

Who you are is what the world needs.

wayofzing.com

We wrote this book to provoke you, inspire you, remind you, and align you.

Think about it. Talk about it. Do something about it.

Share it with others, for others.

Join our Caravan at wayofzing.com. Read stories about people living as Ventures of One. Explore exercises and practices to calibrate your *Zing* Compass, and travel your Pursuits. Share your *Zing* adventures with us.

Let's align the world.

CPSIA information can be obtained
at www.ICGtesting.com
Printed in the USA
FSOW01n2318290817
37984FS

9 780999 262610